MW00490703

ZEN COLORING

THE ULTIMATE COLLECTION

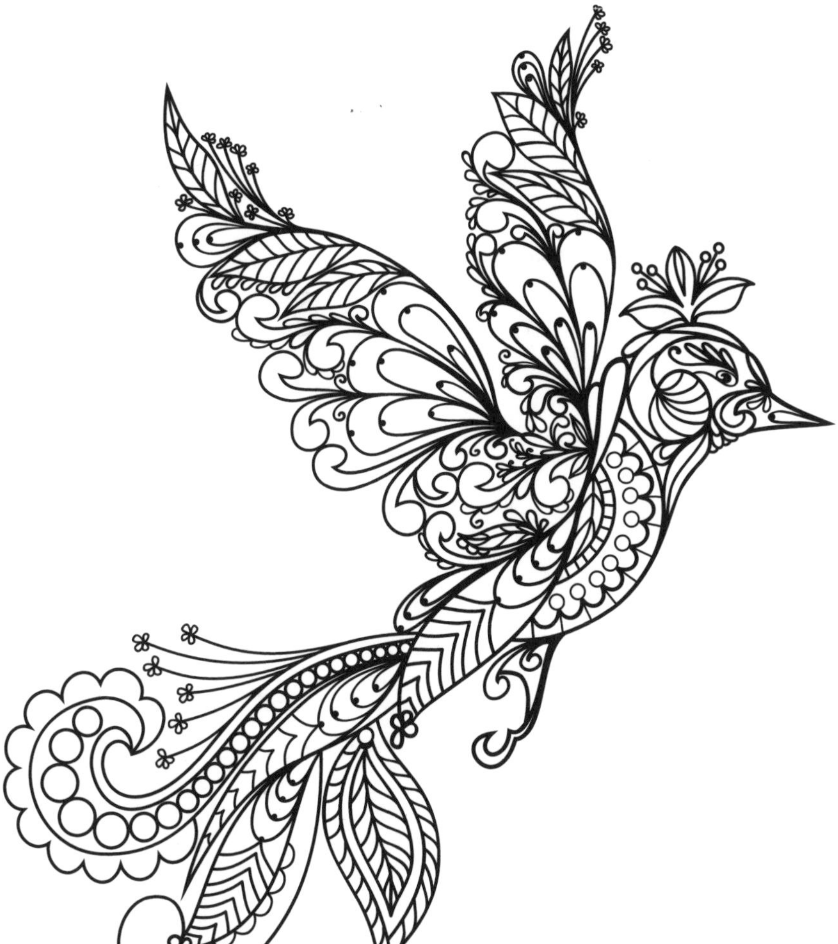

THE GUILD OF MASTER CRAFTSMAN PUBLICATIONS

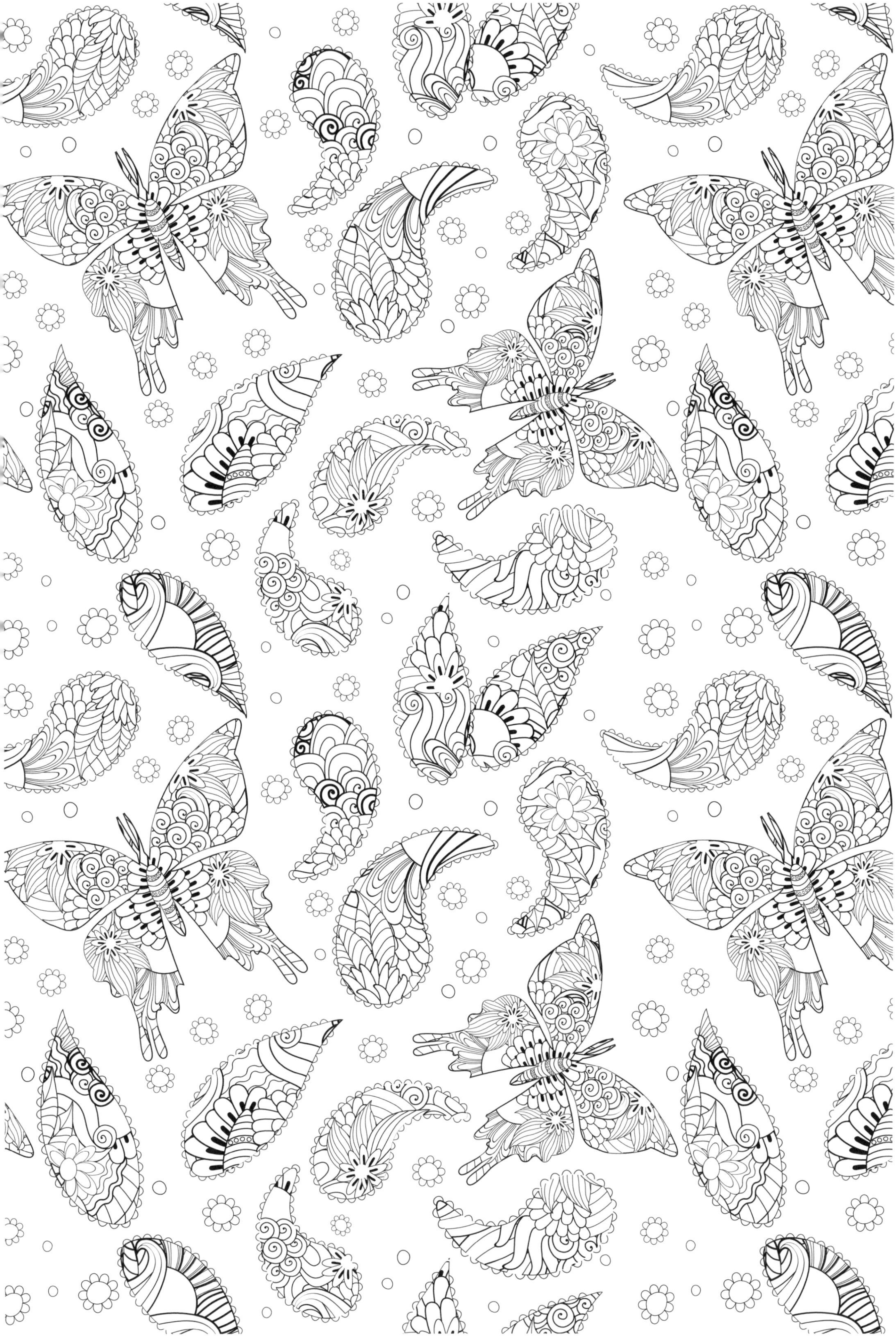

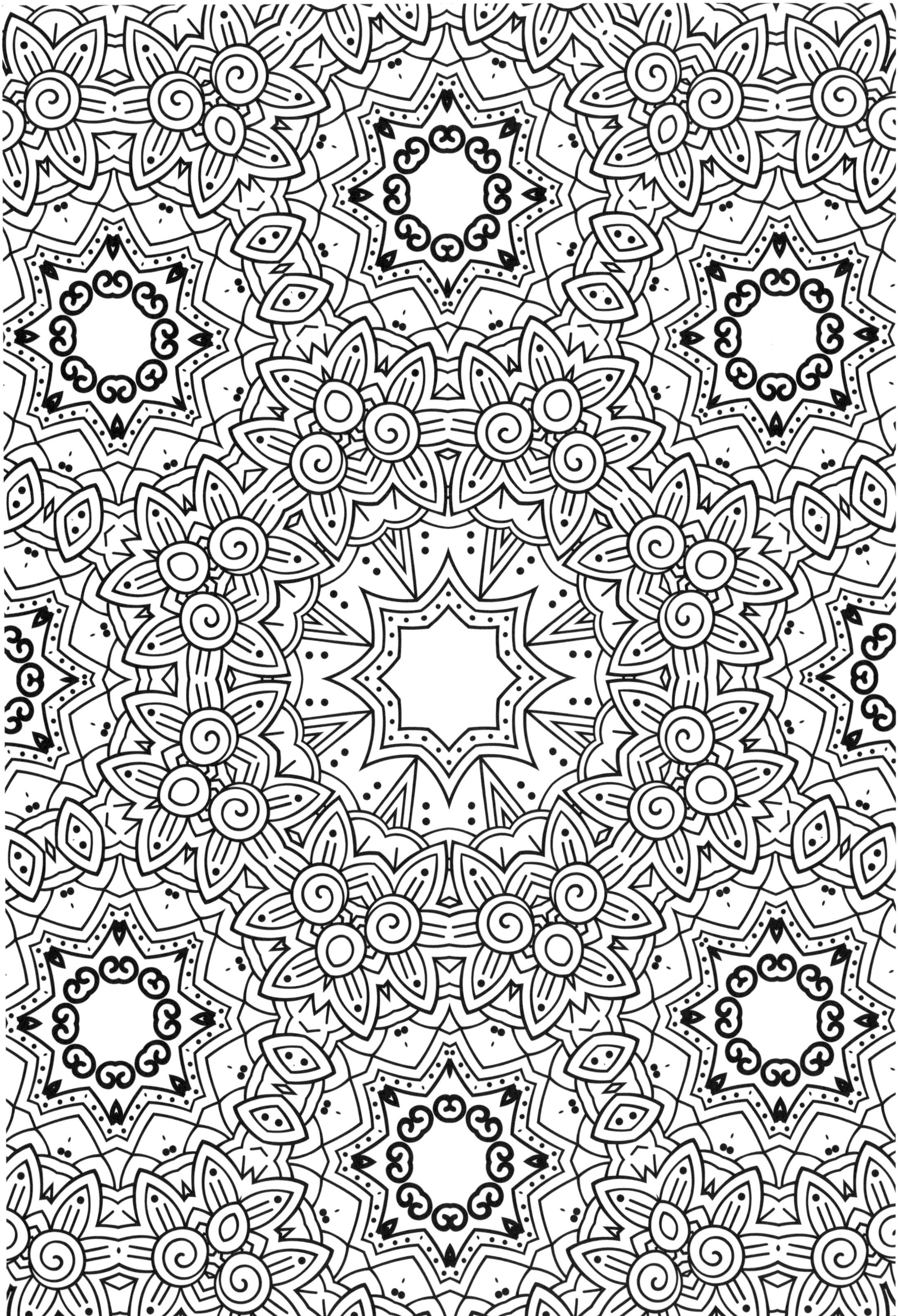

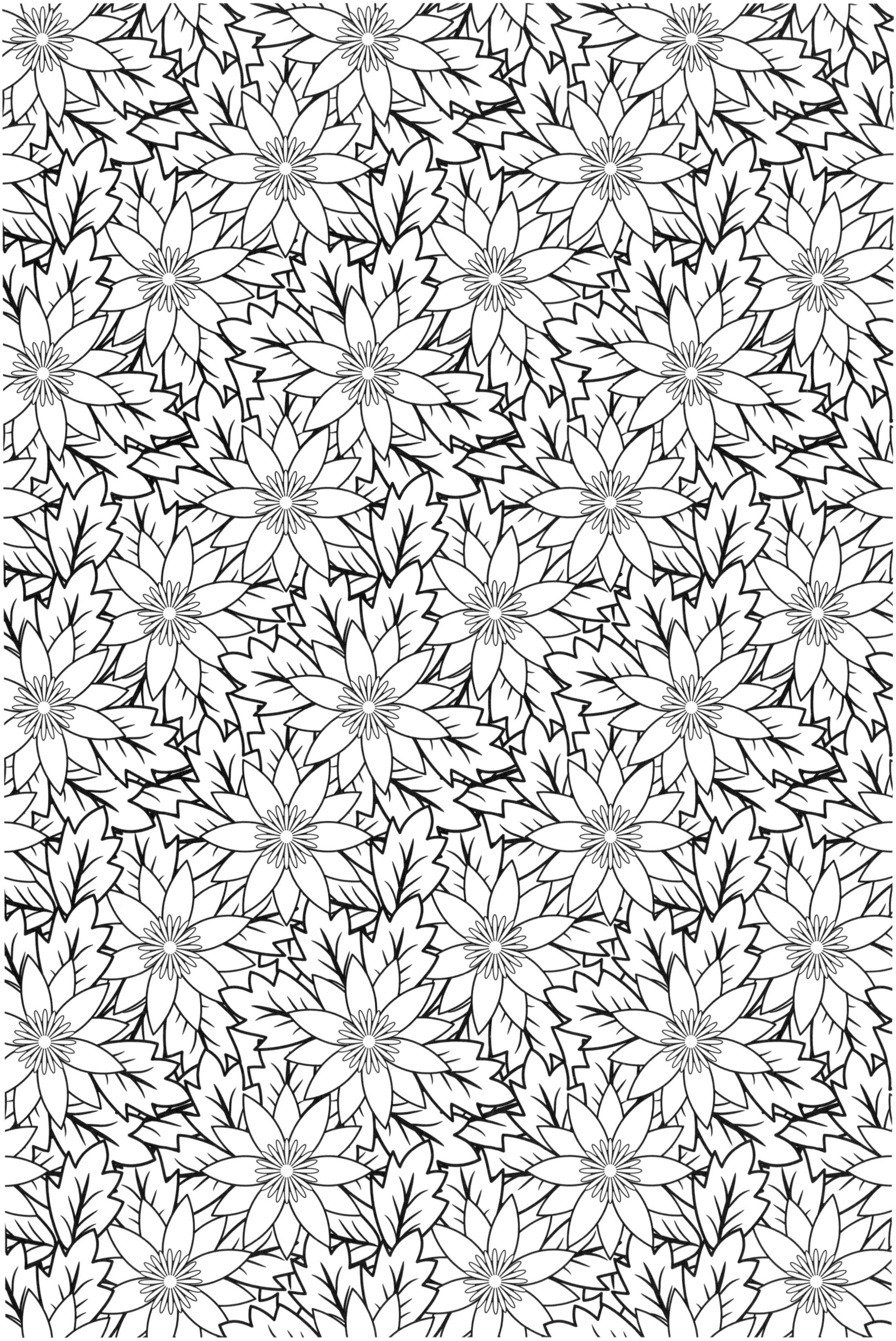

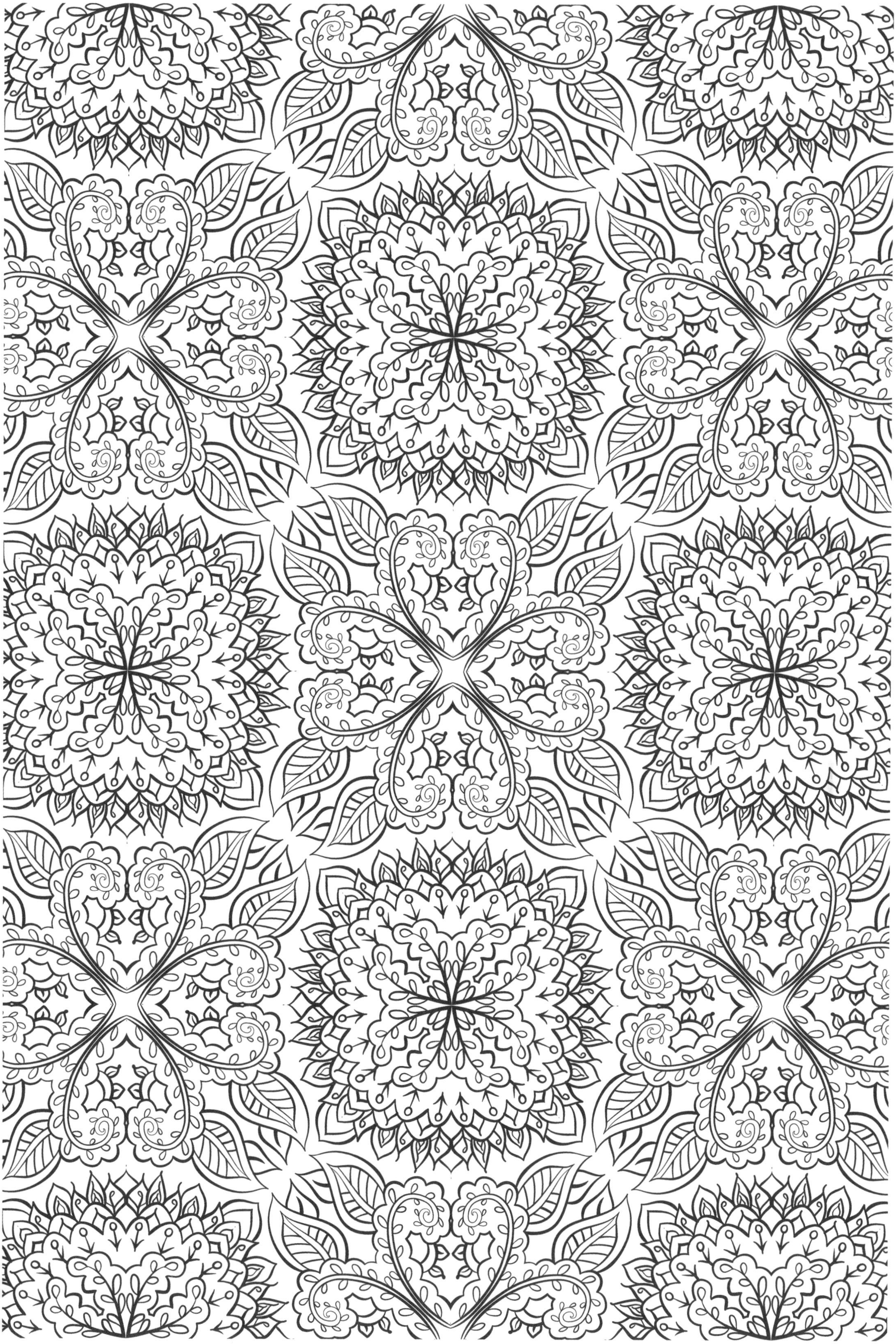

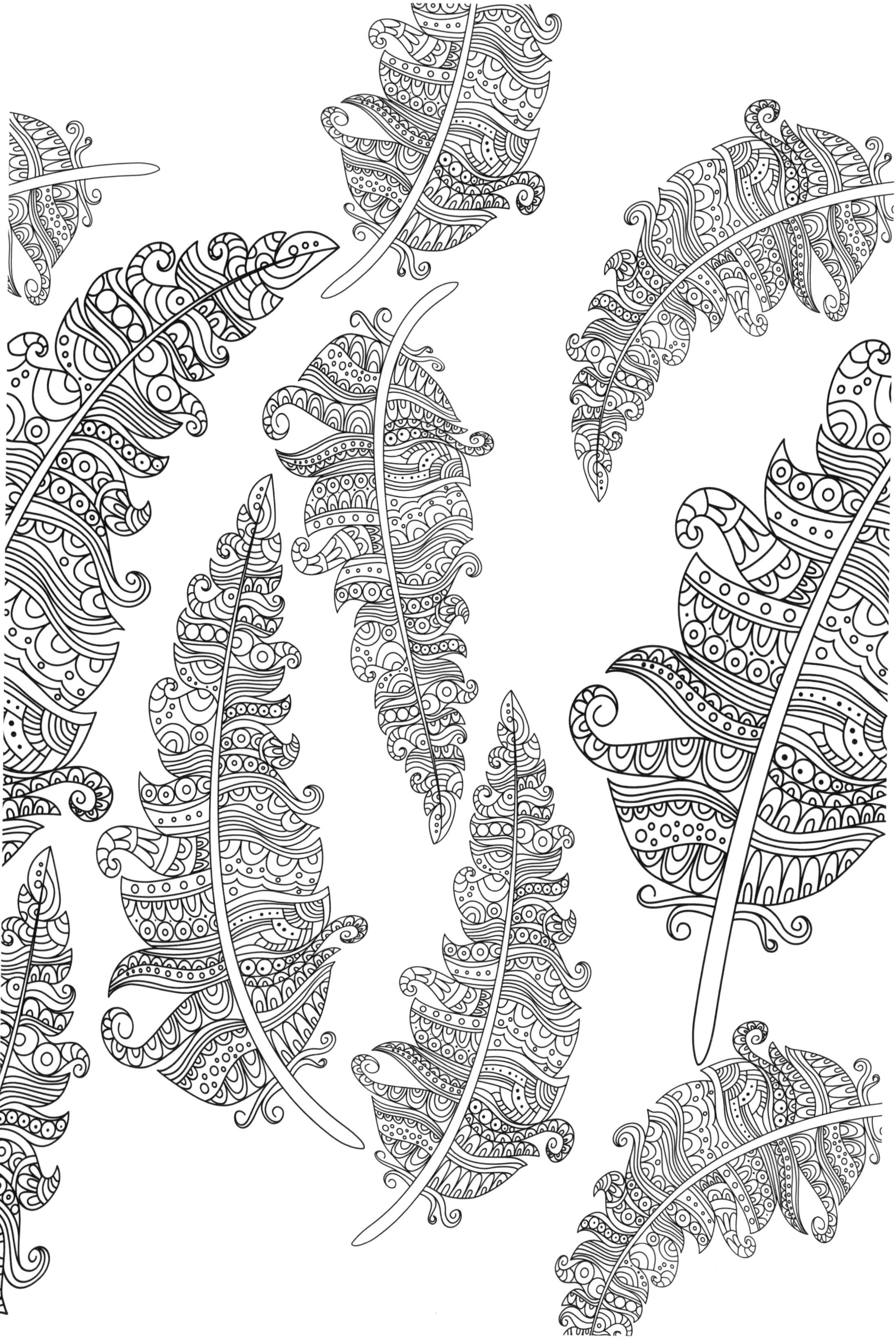

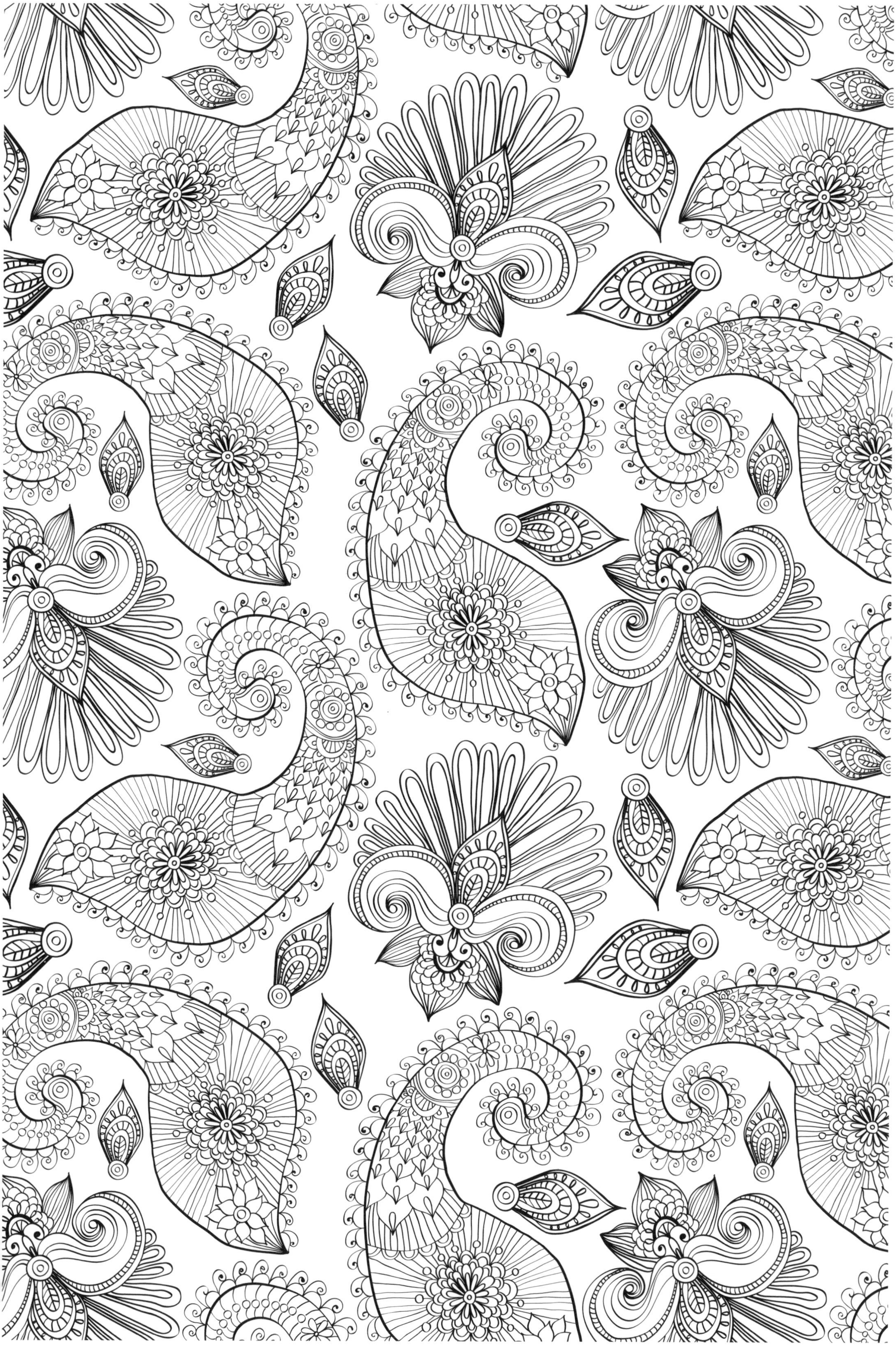

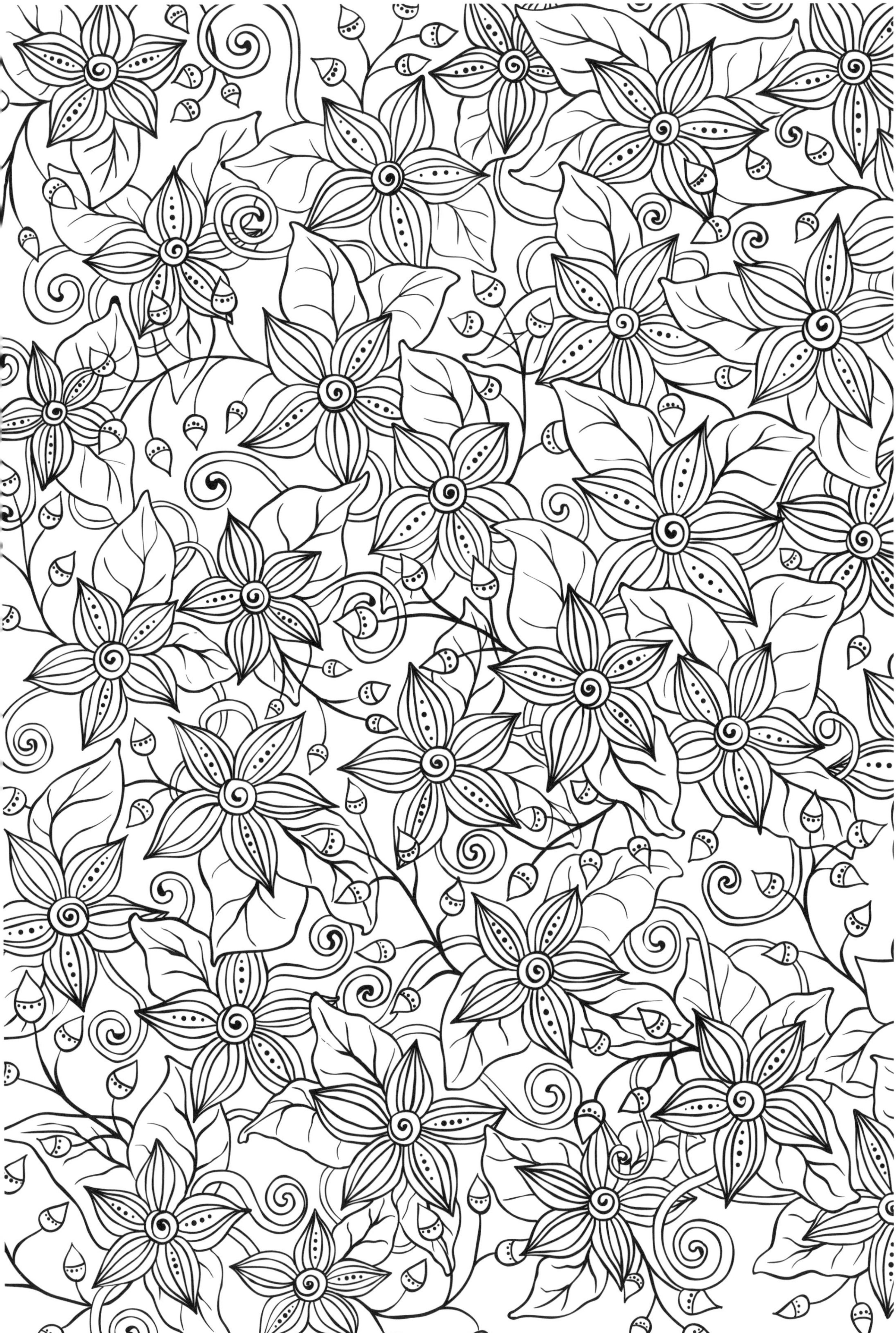

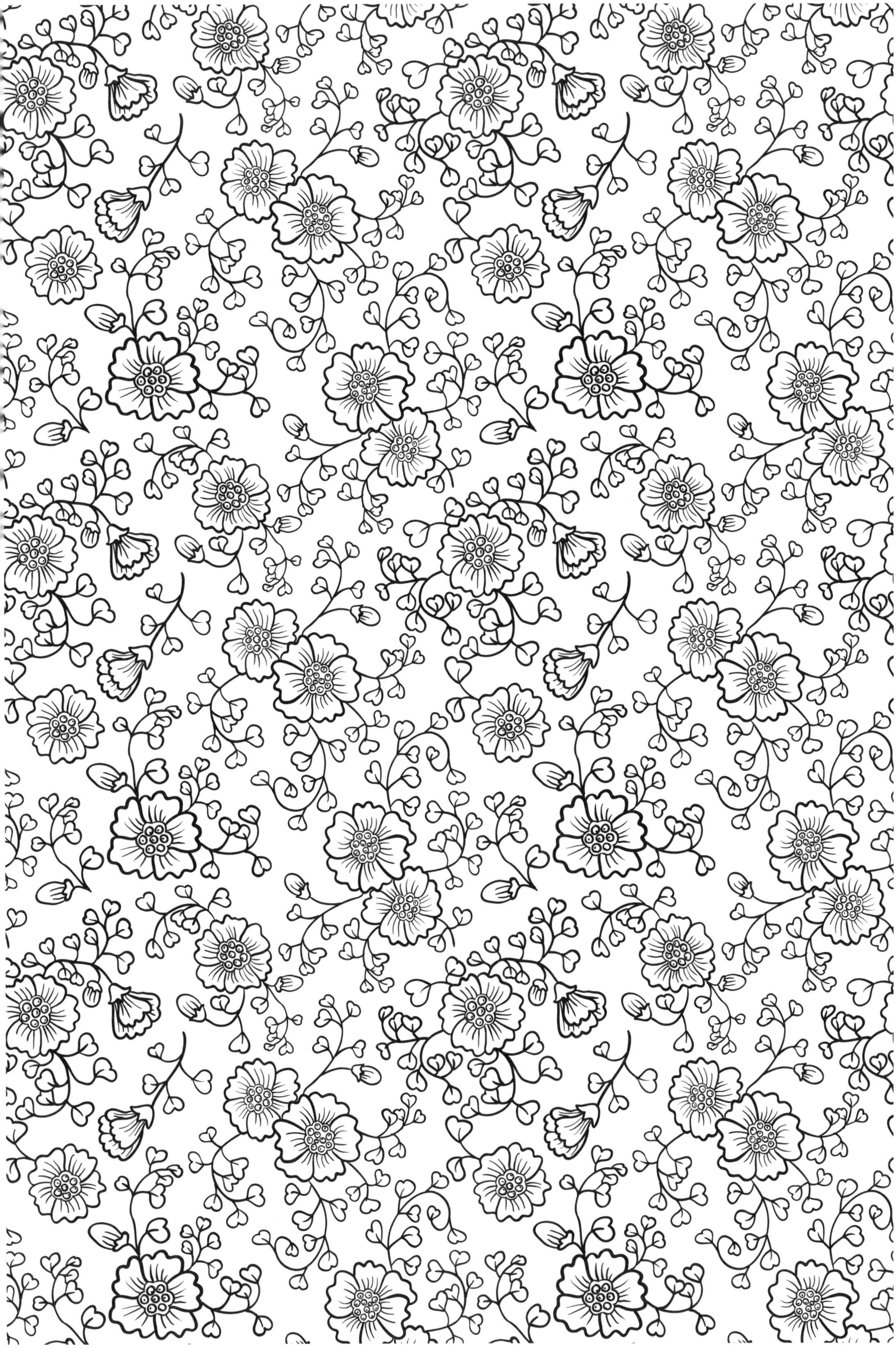

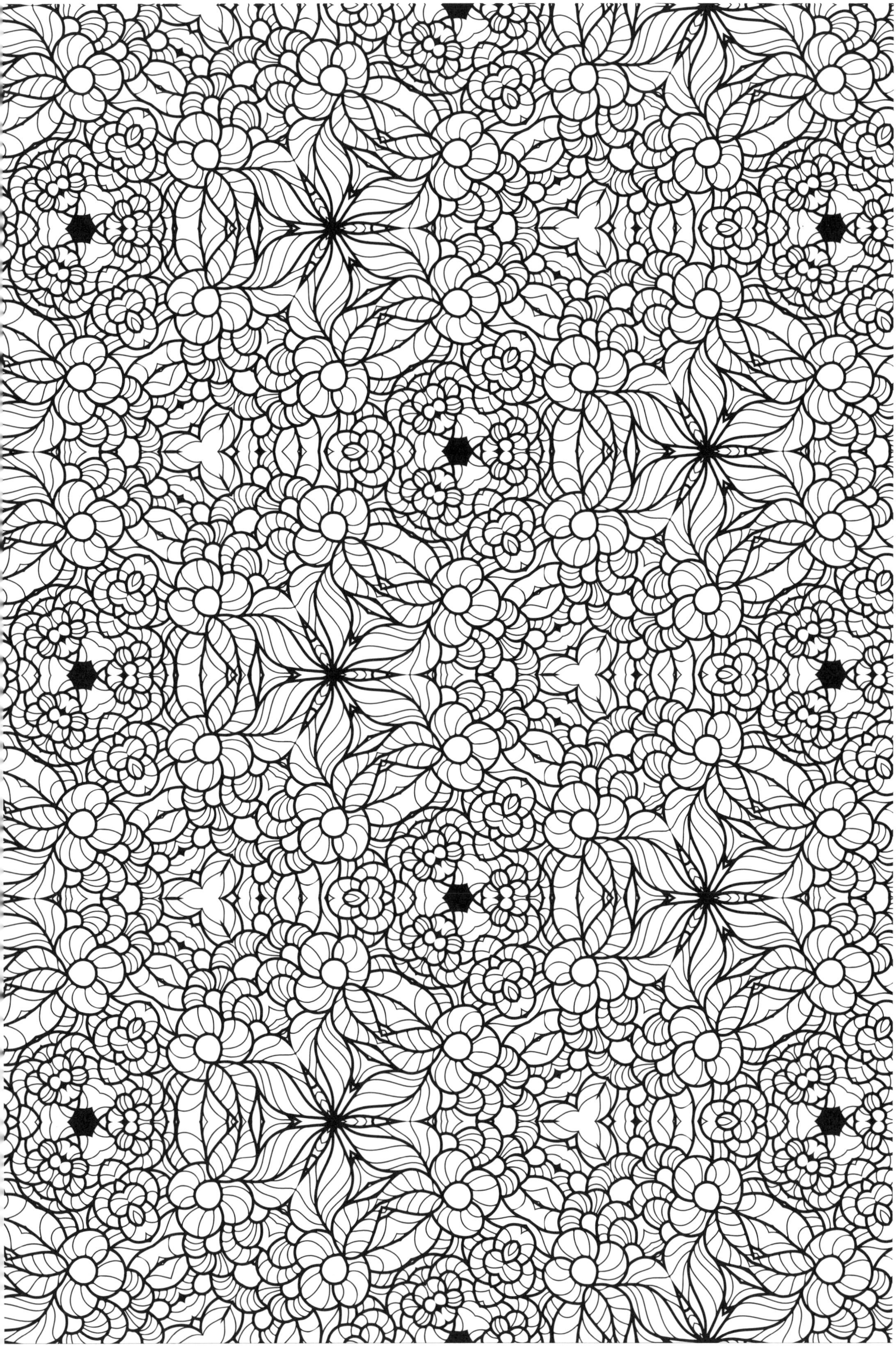

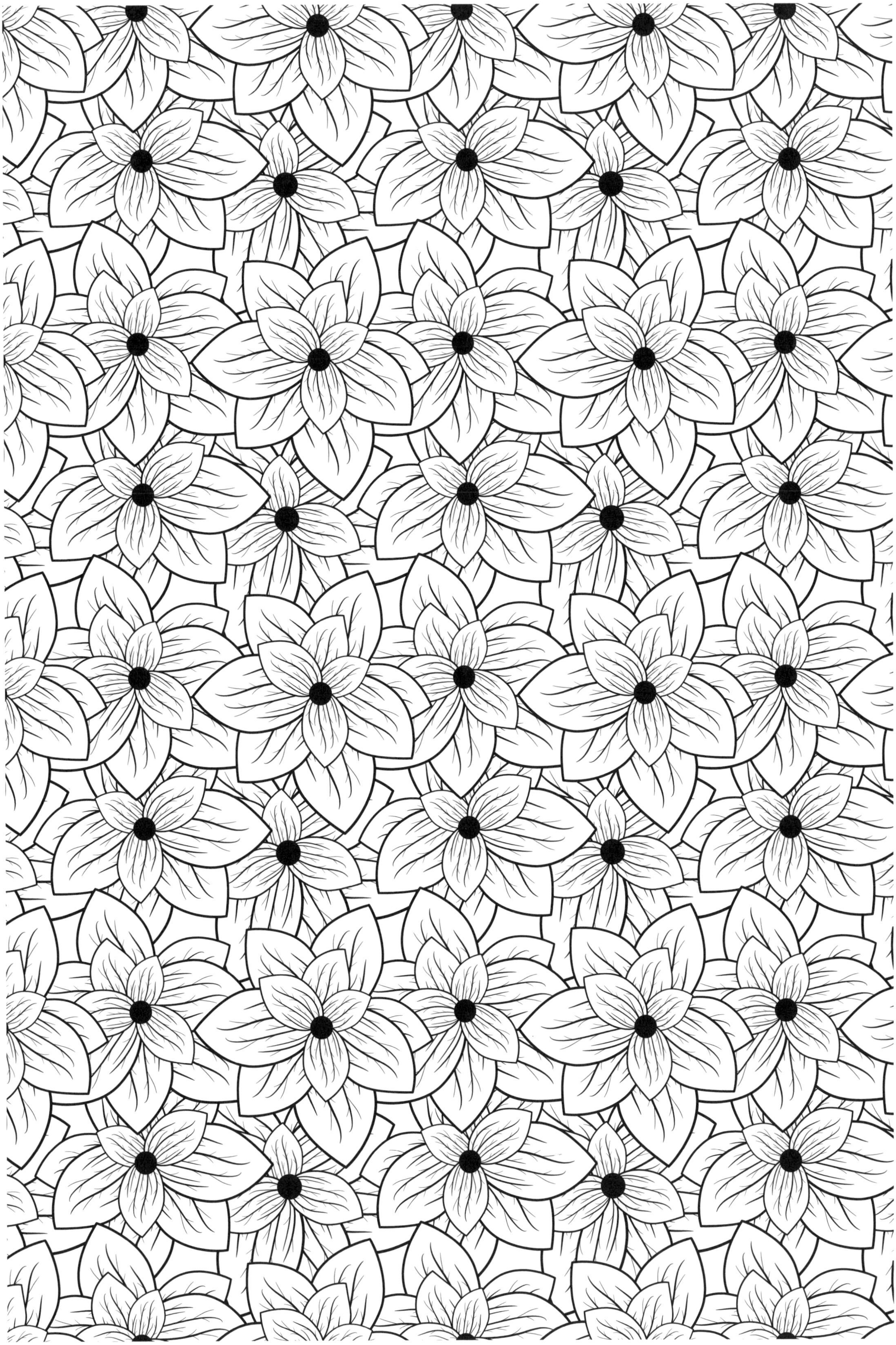

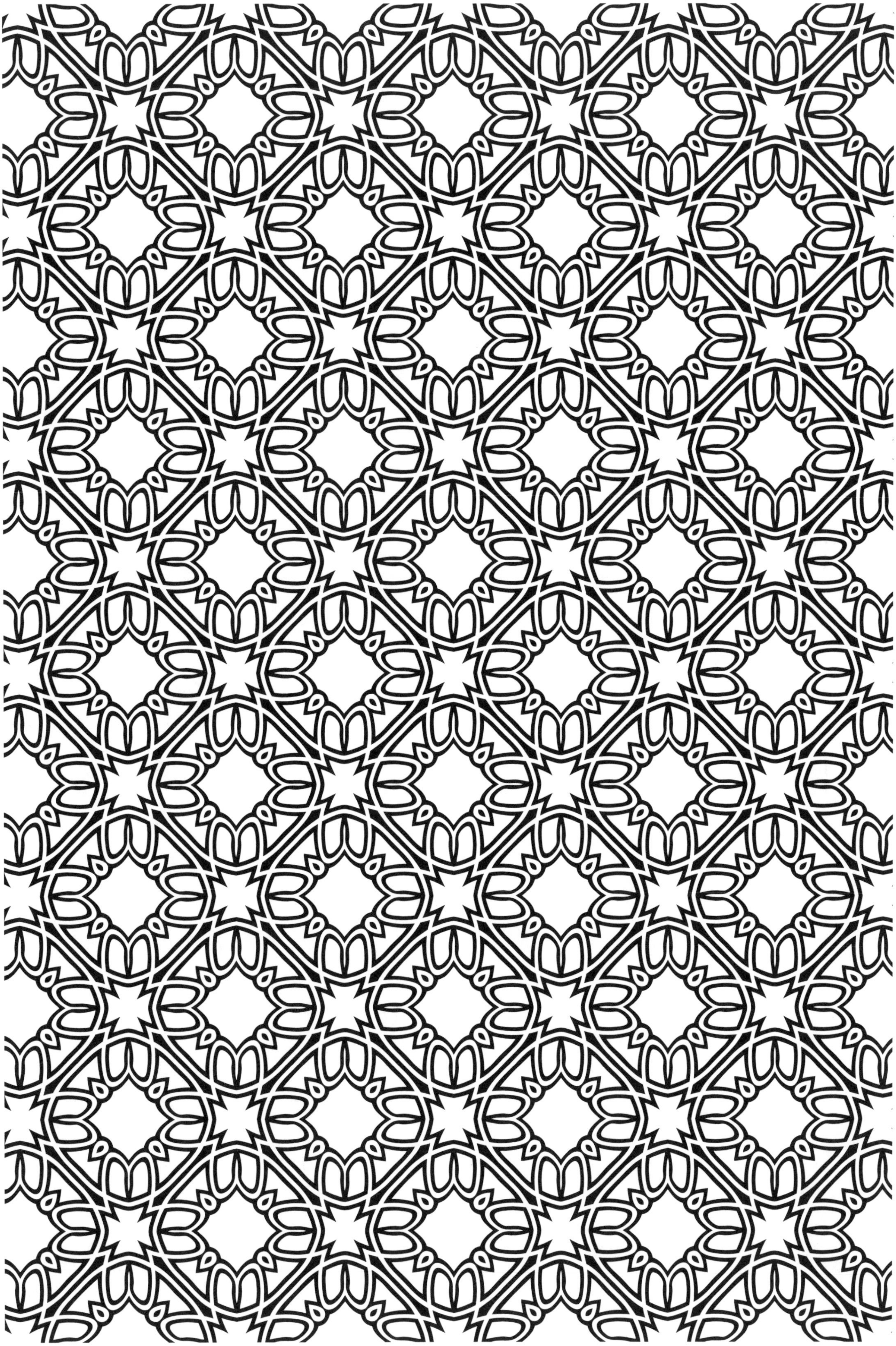

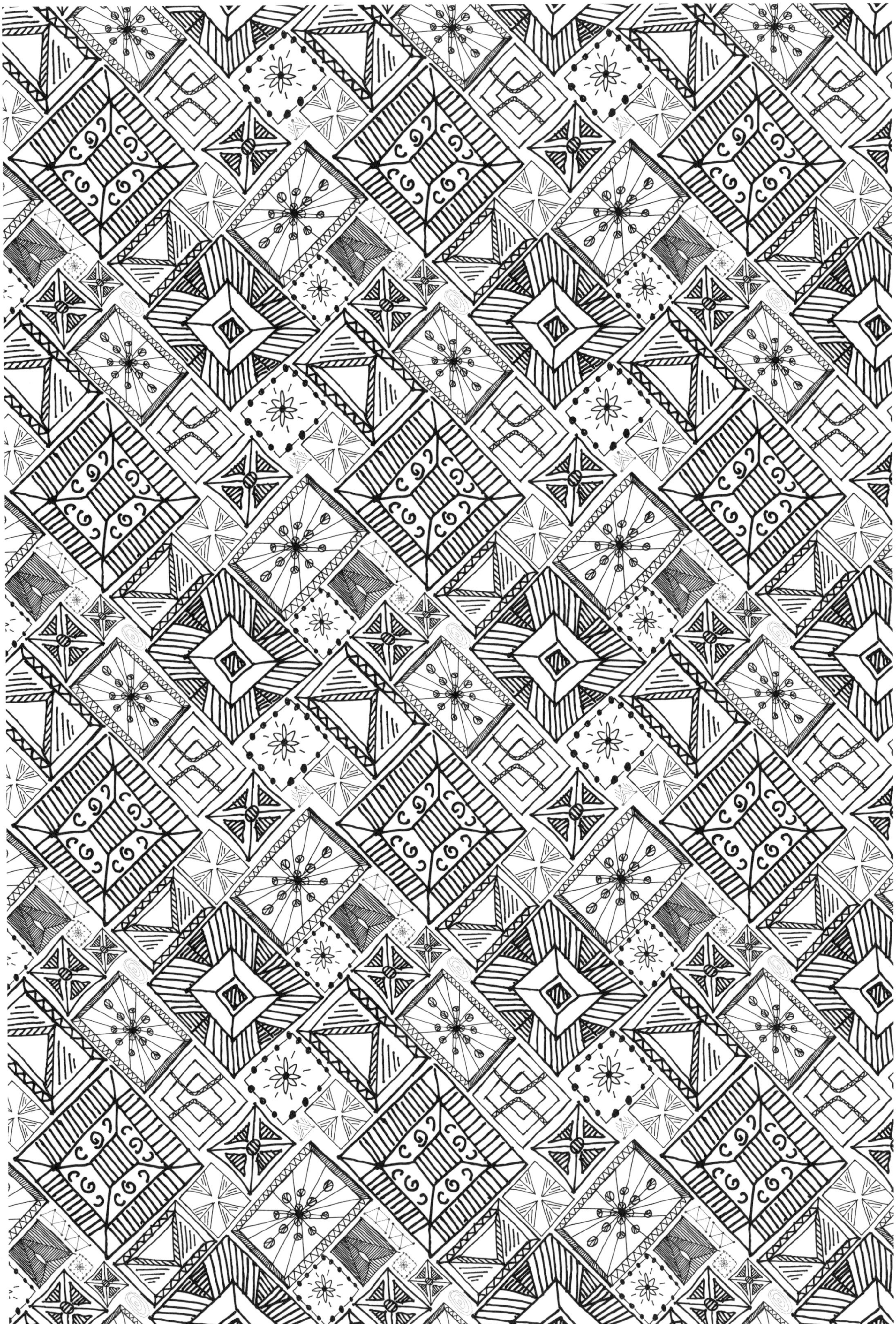

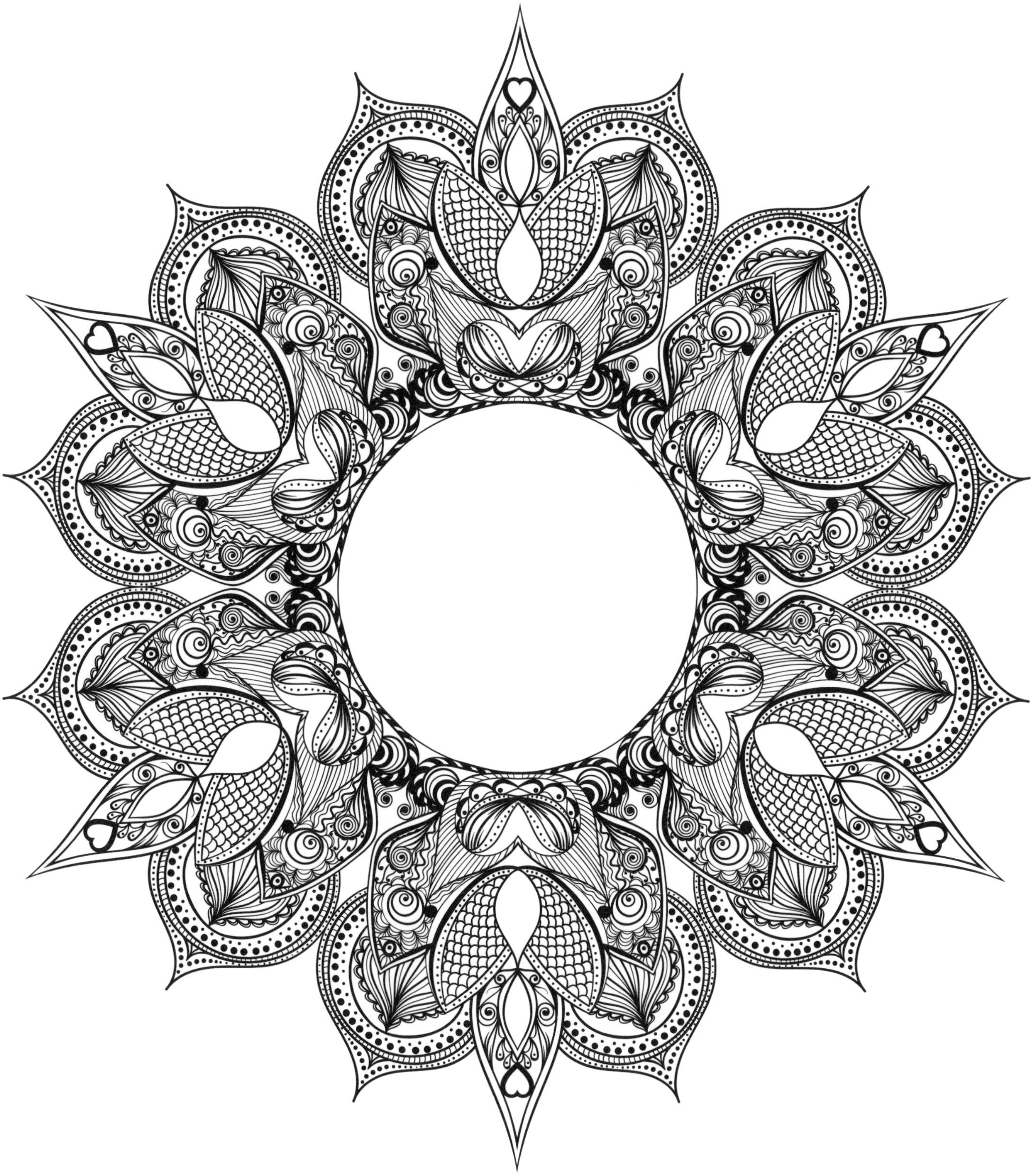

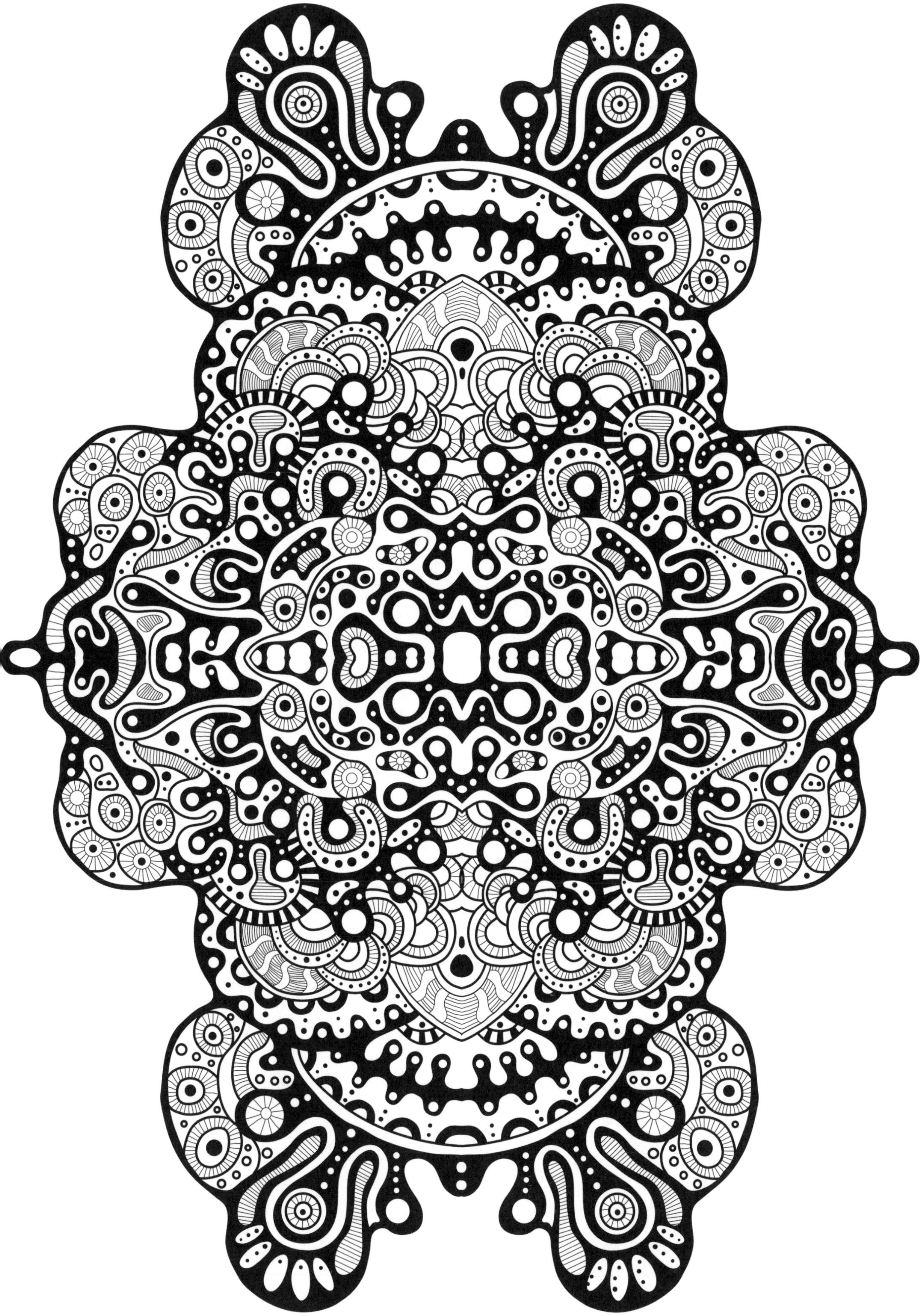

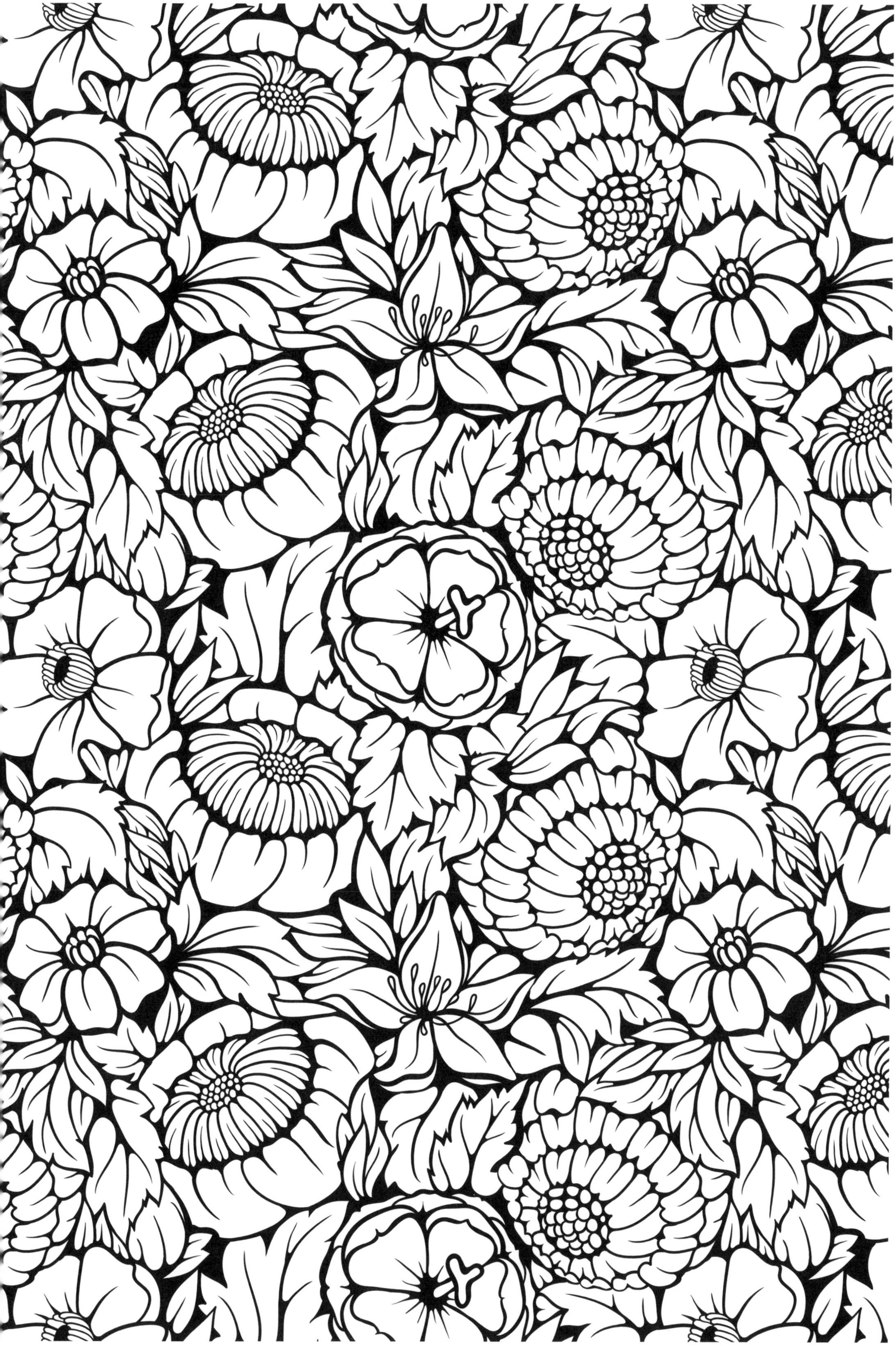

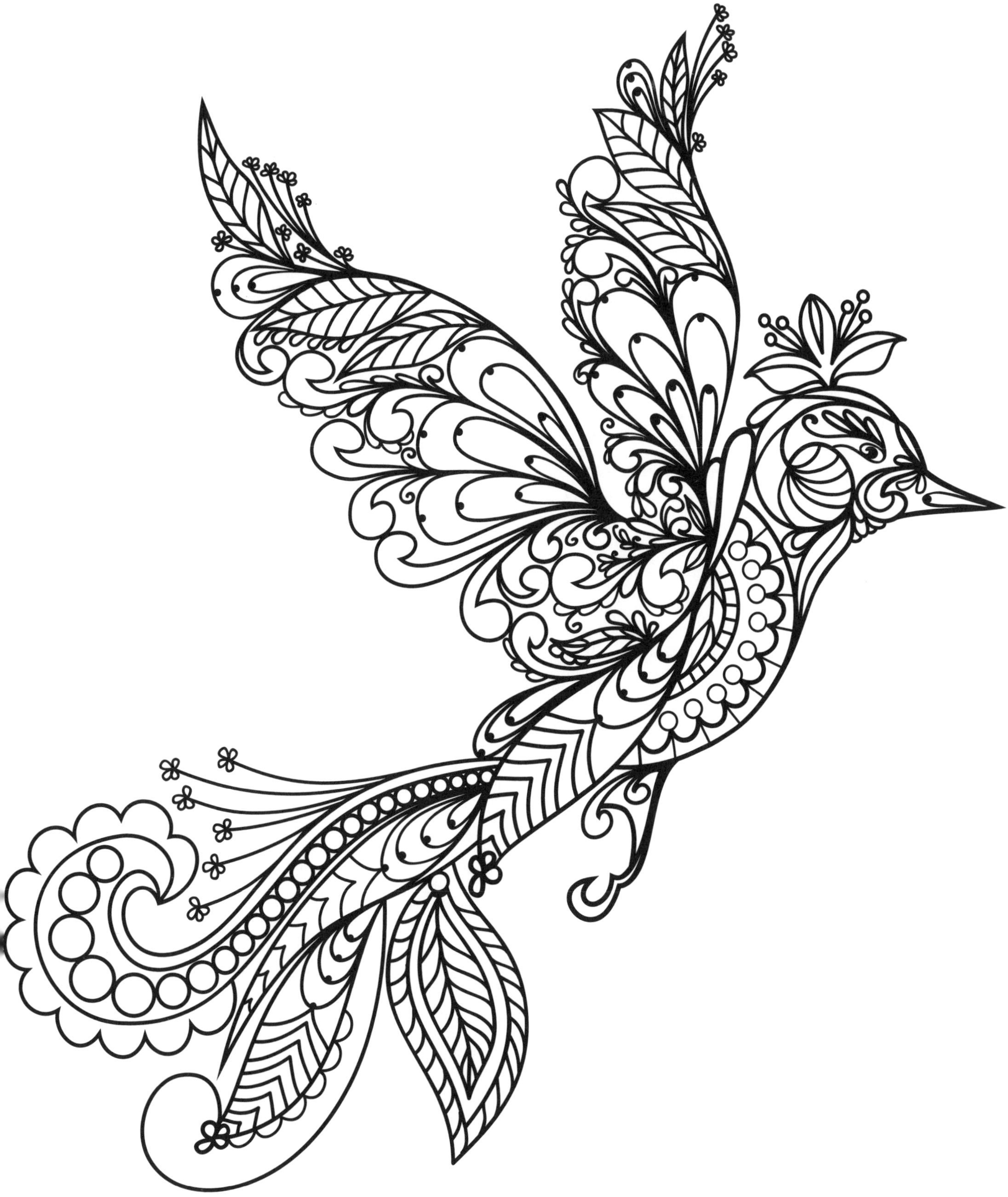

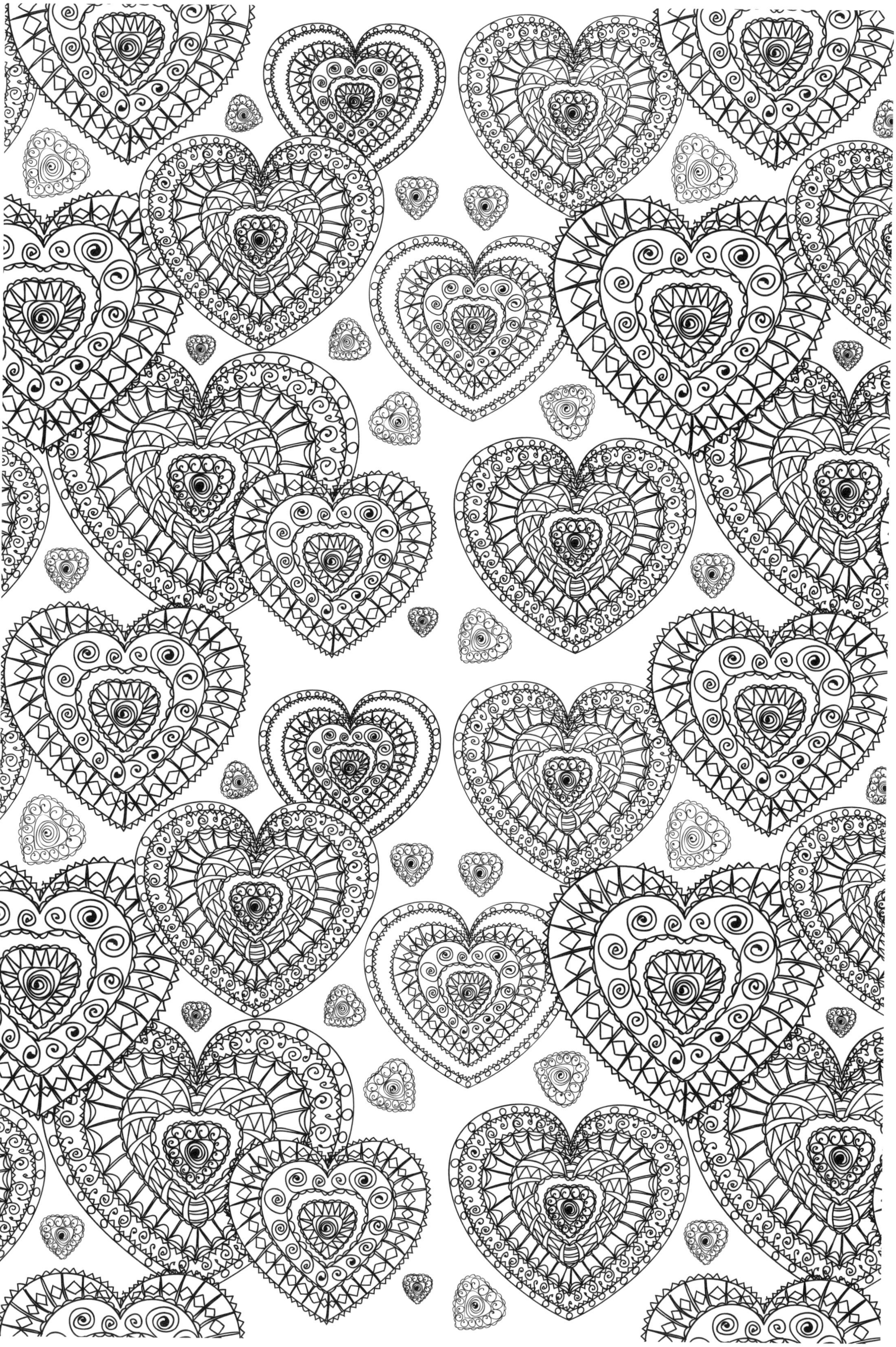

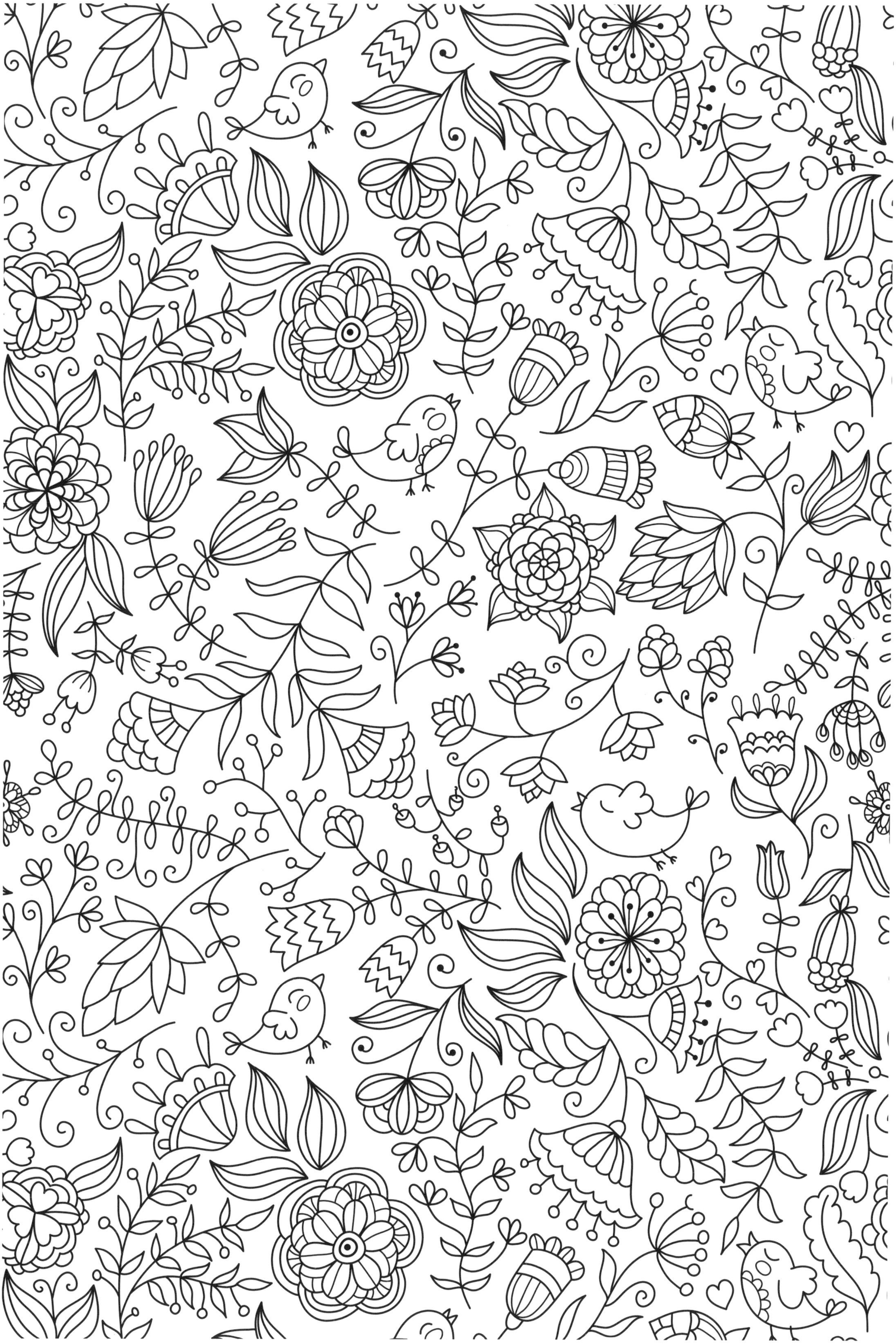

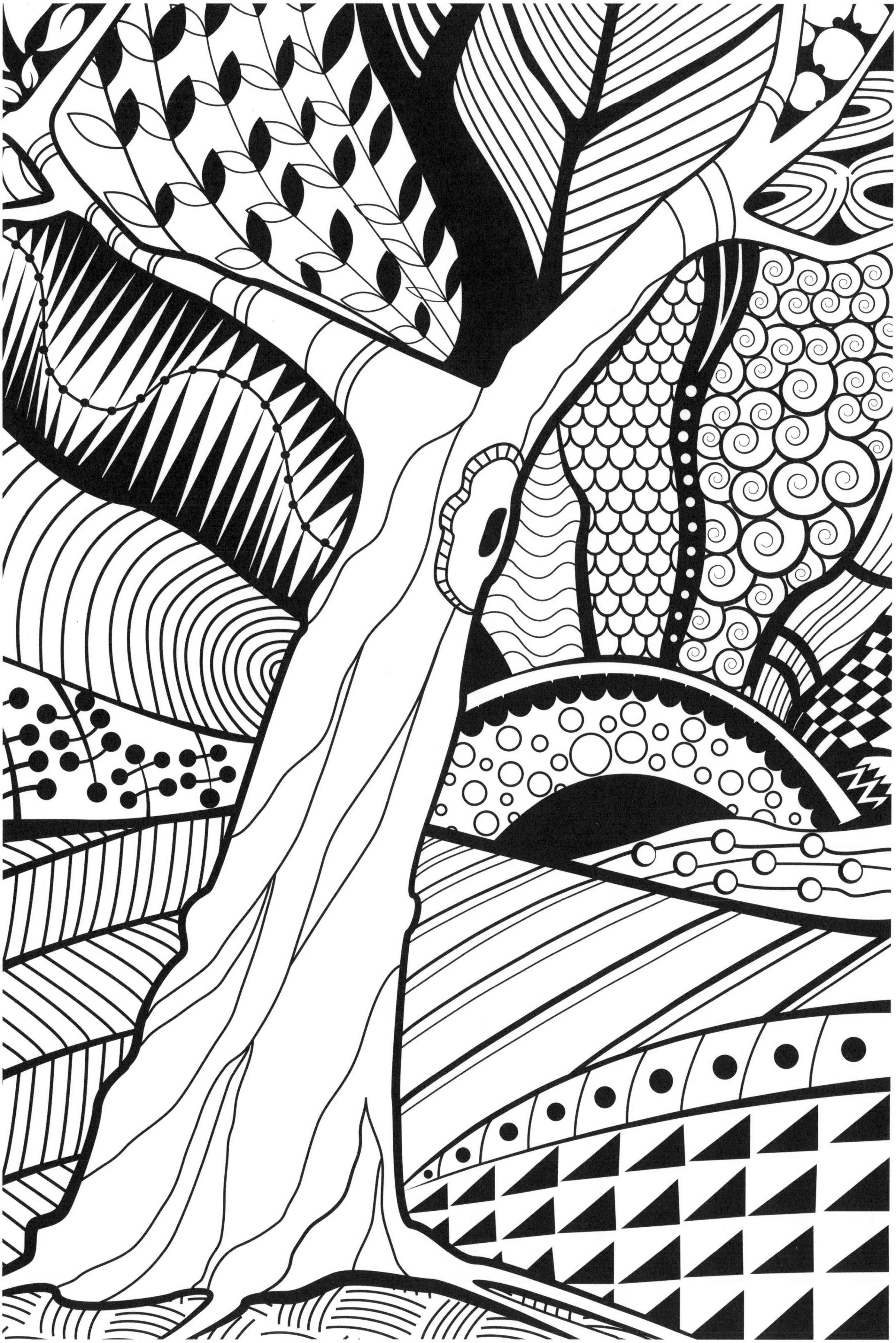

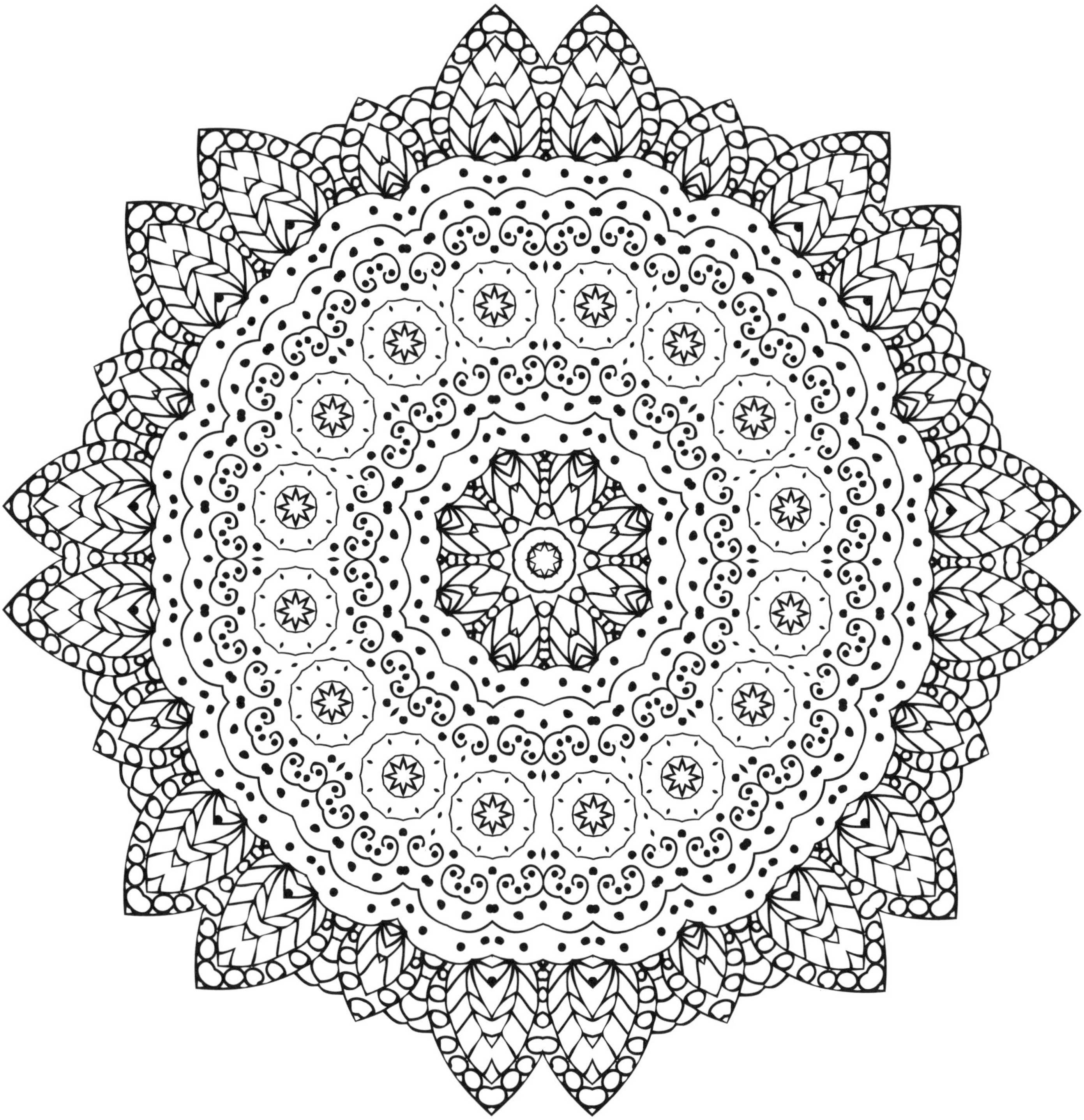

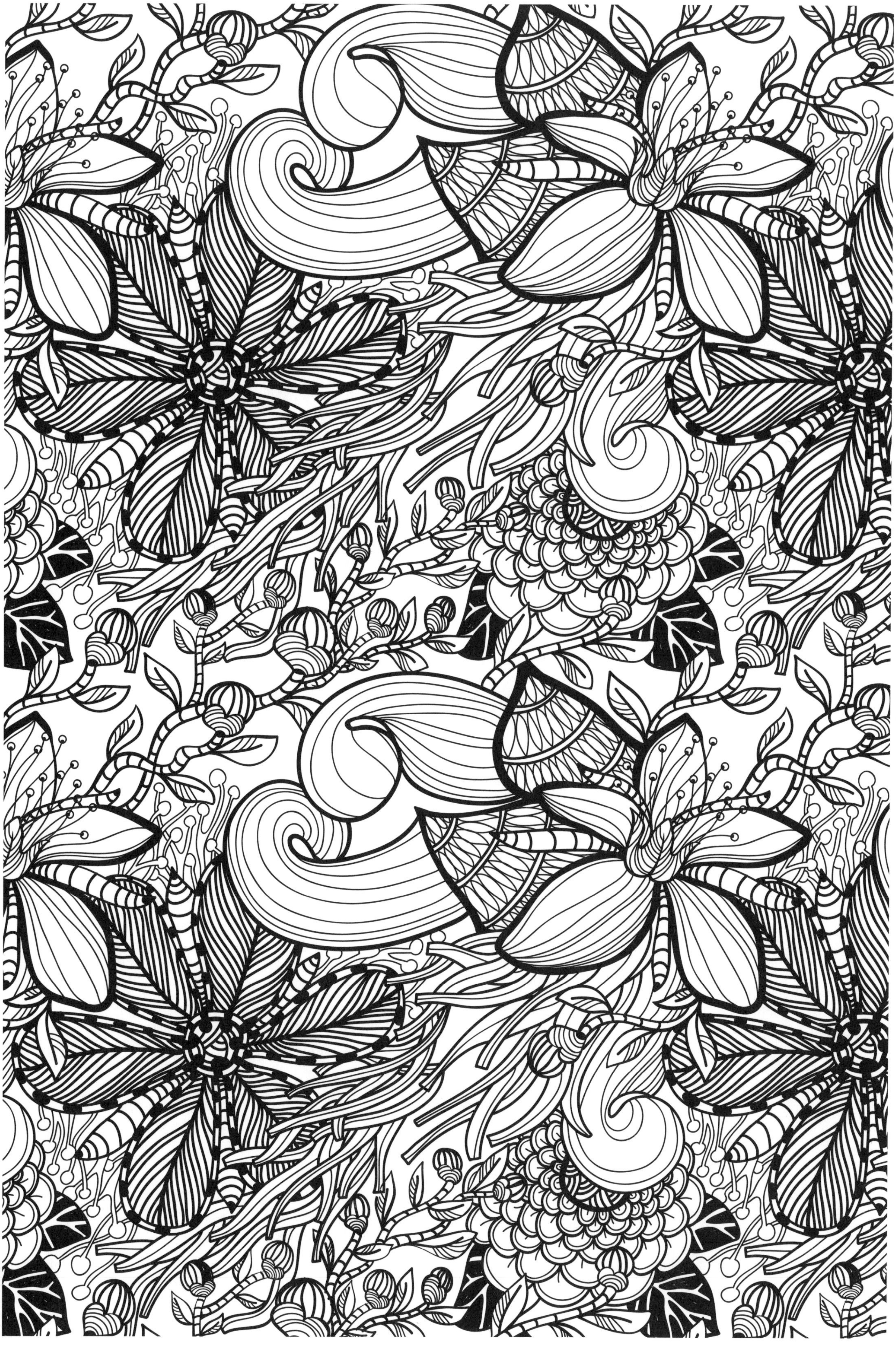

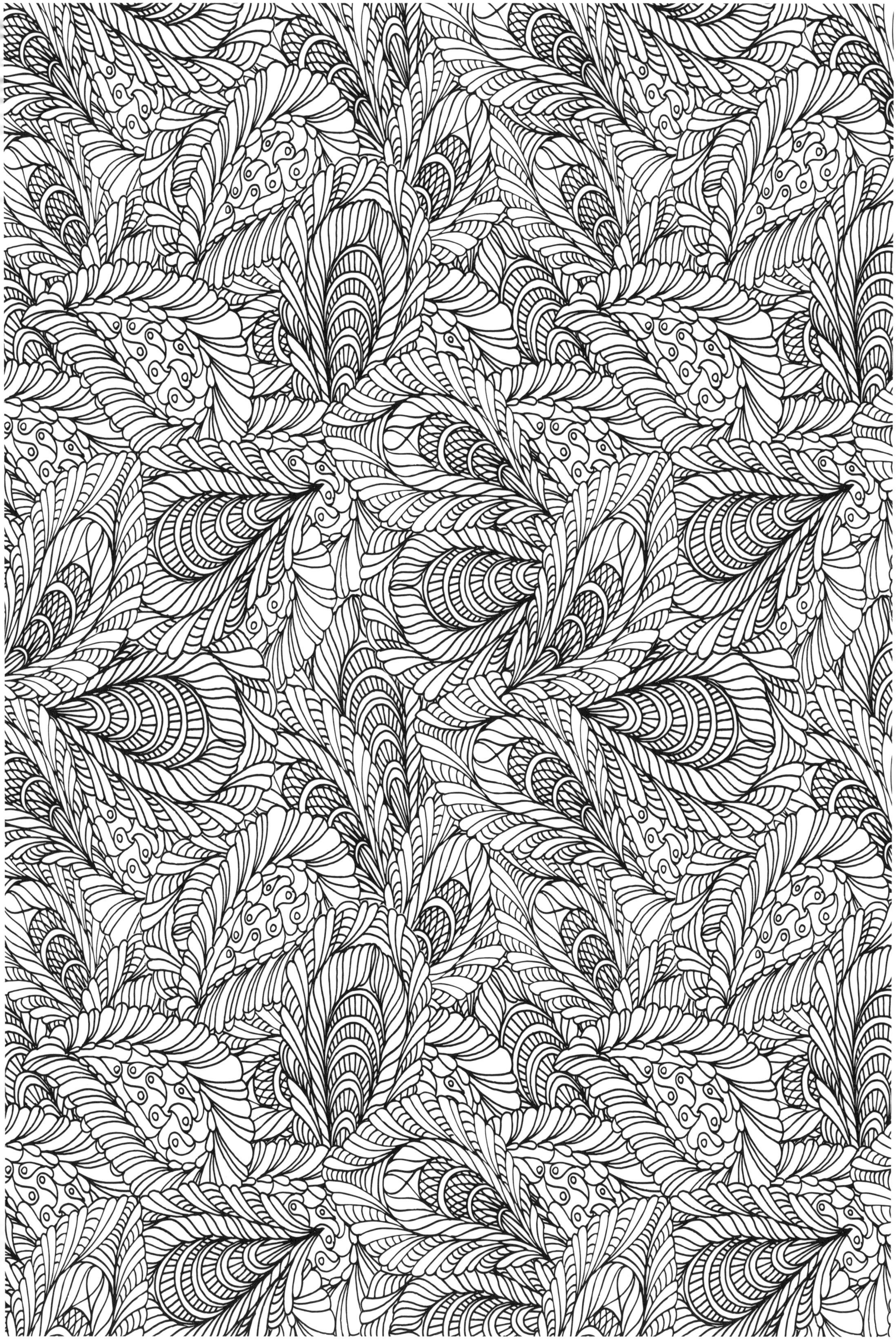

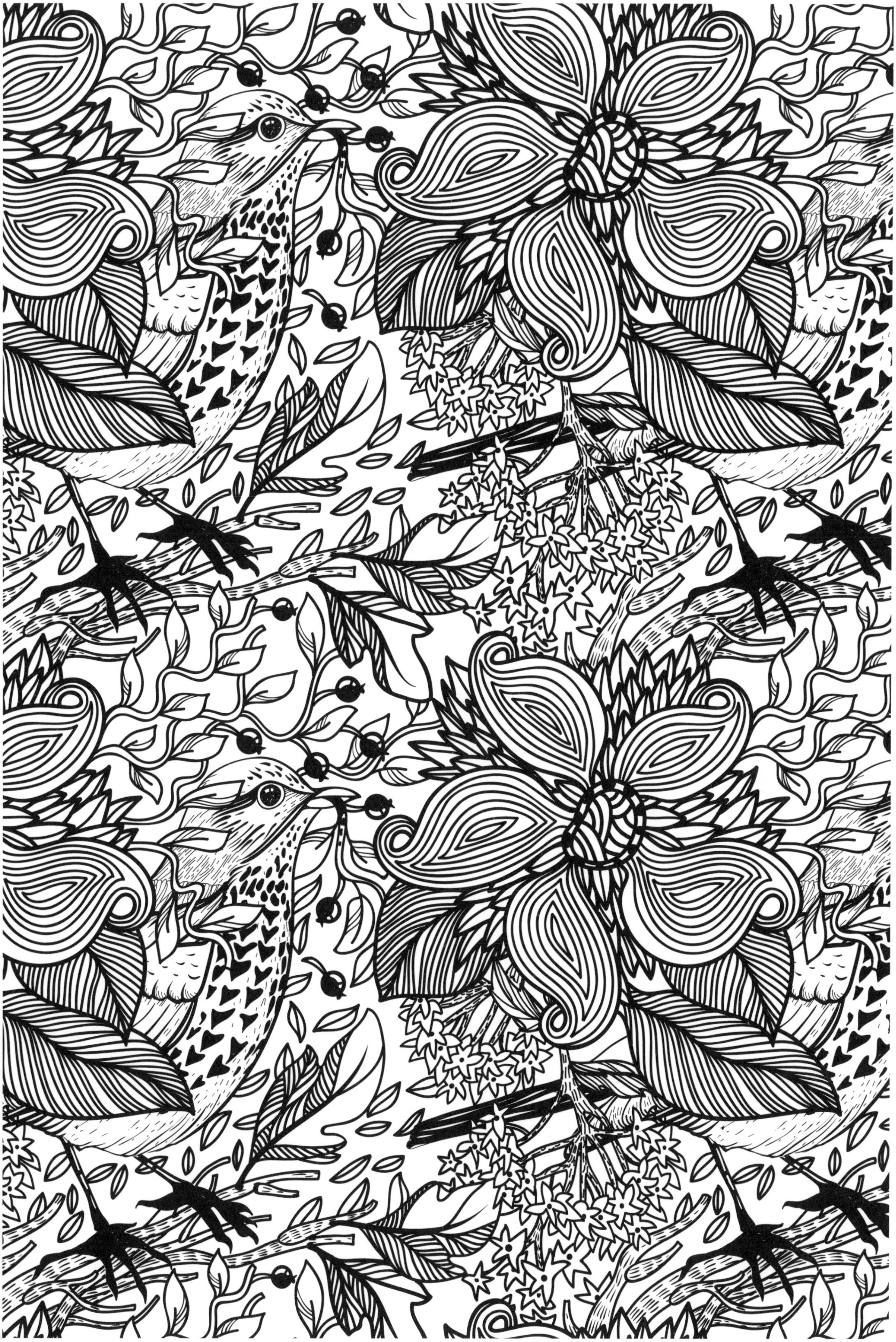

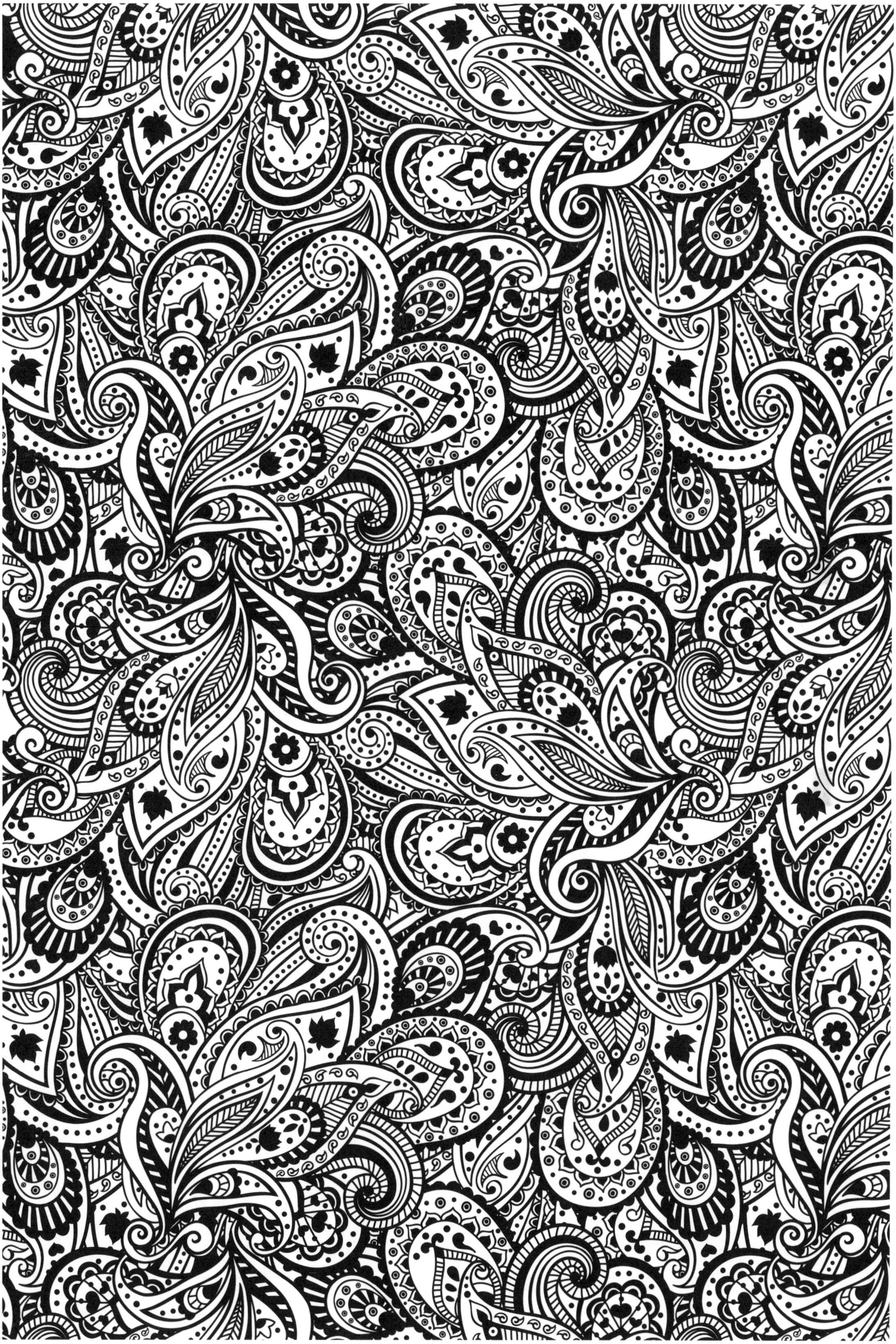

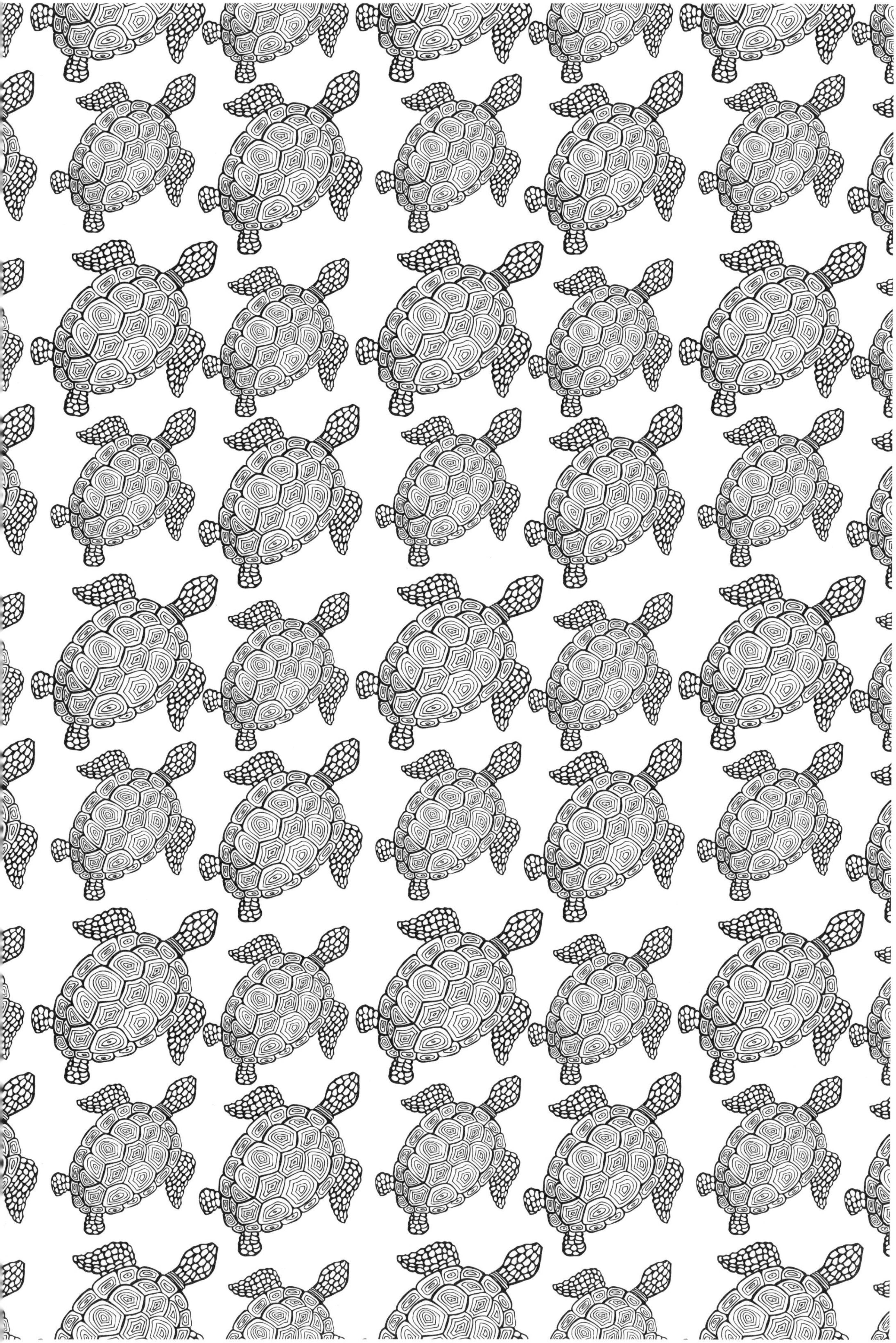

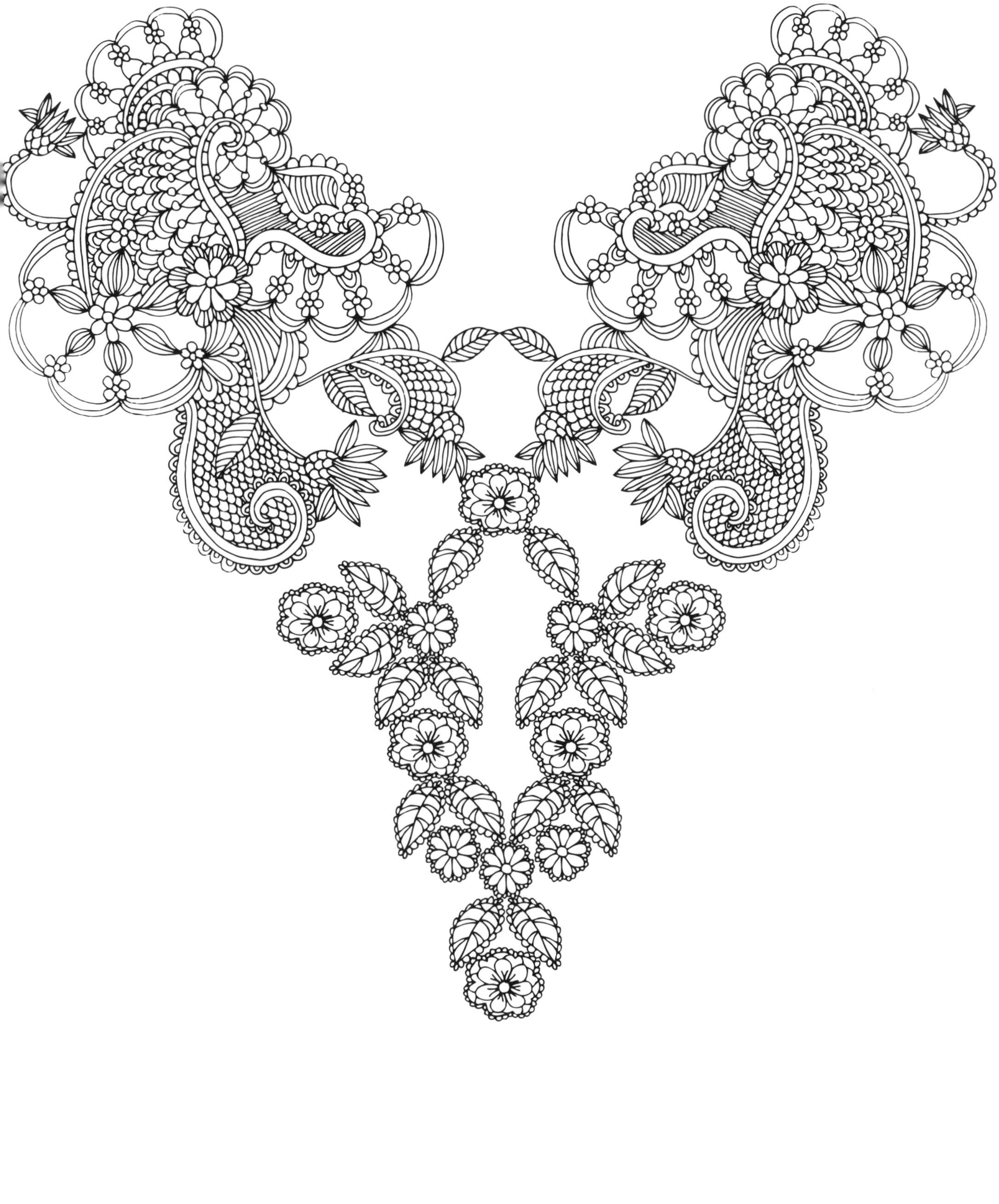

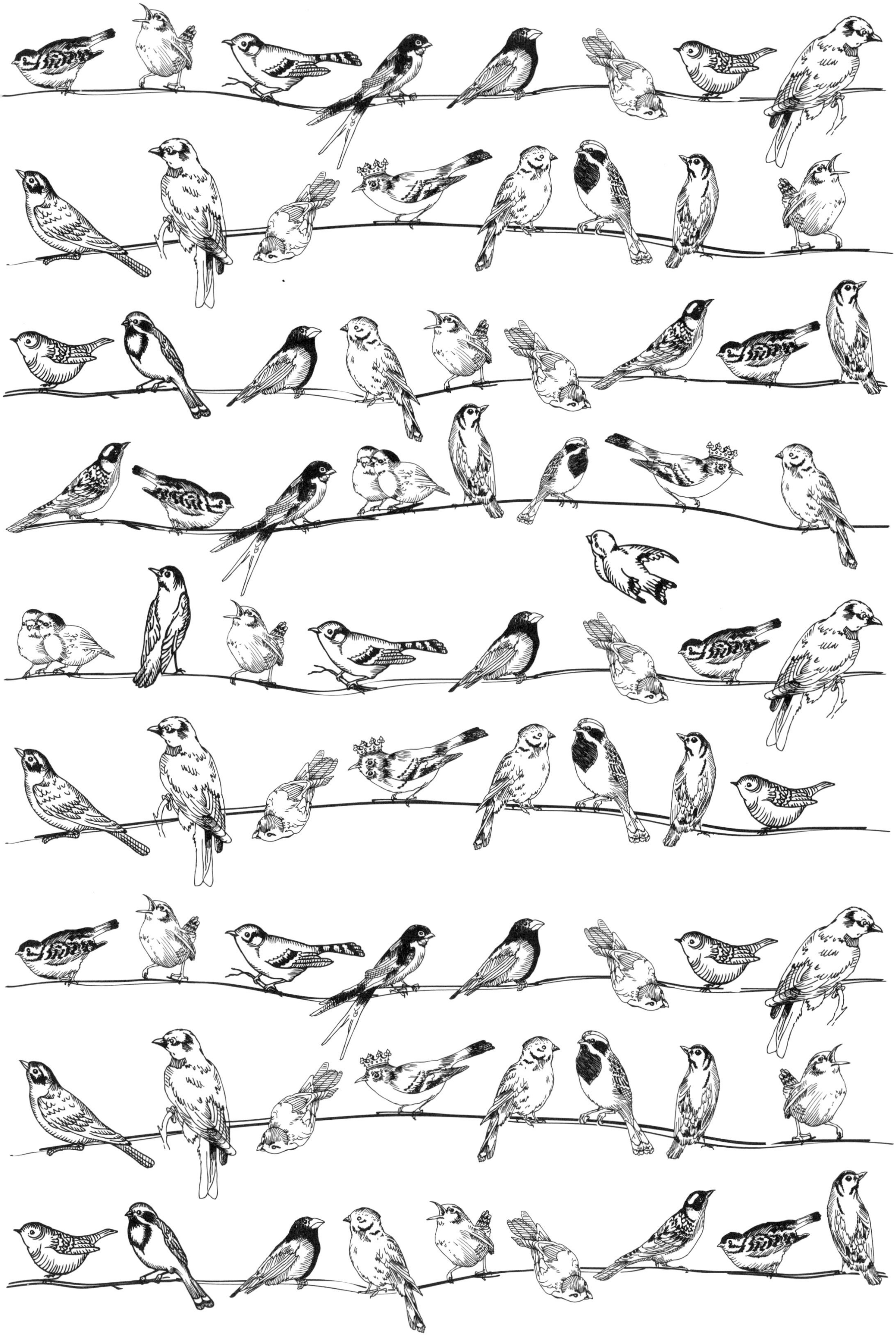

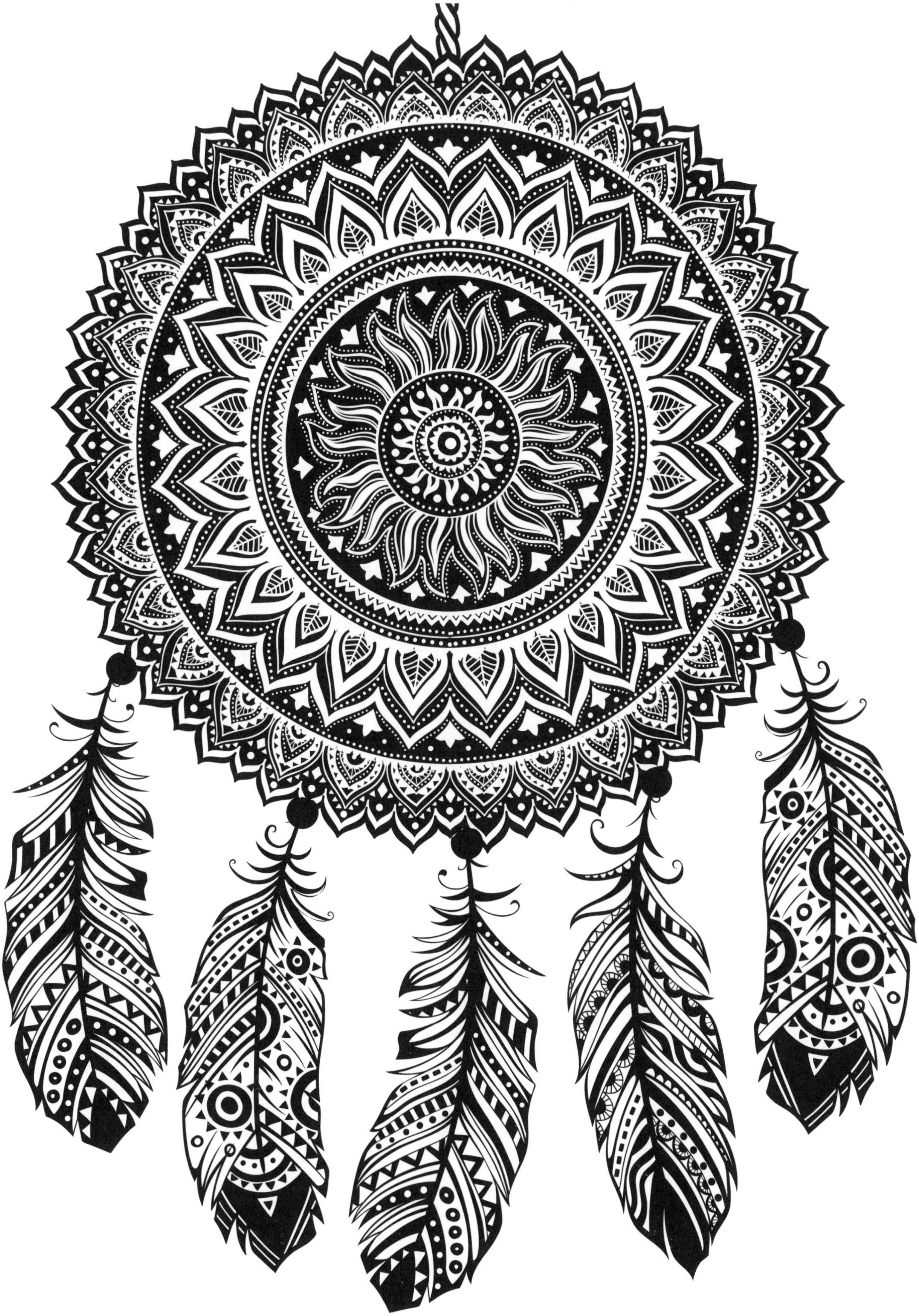

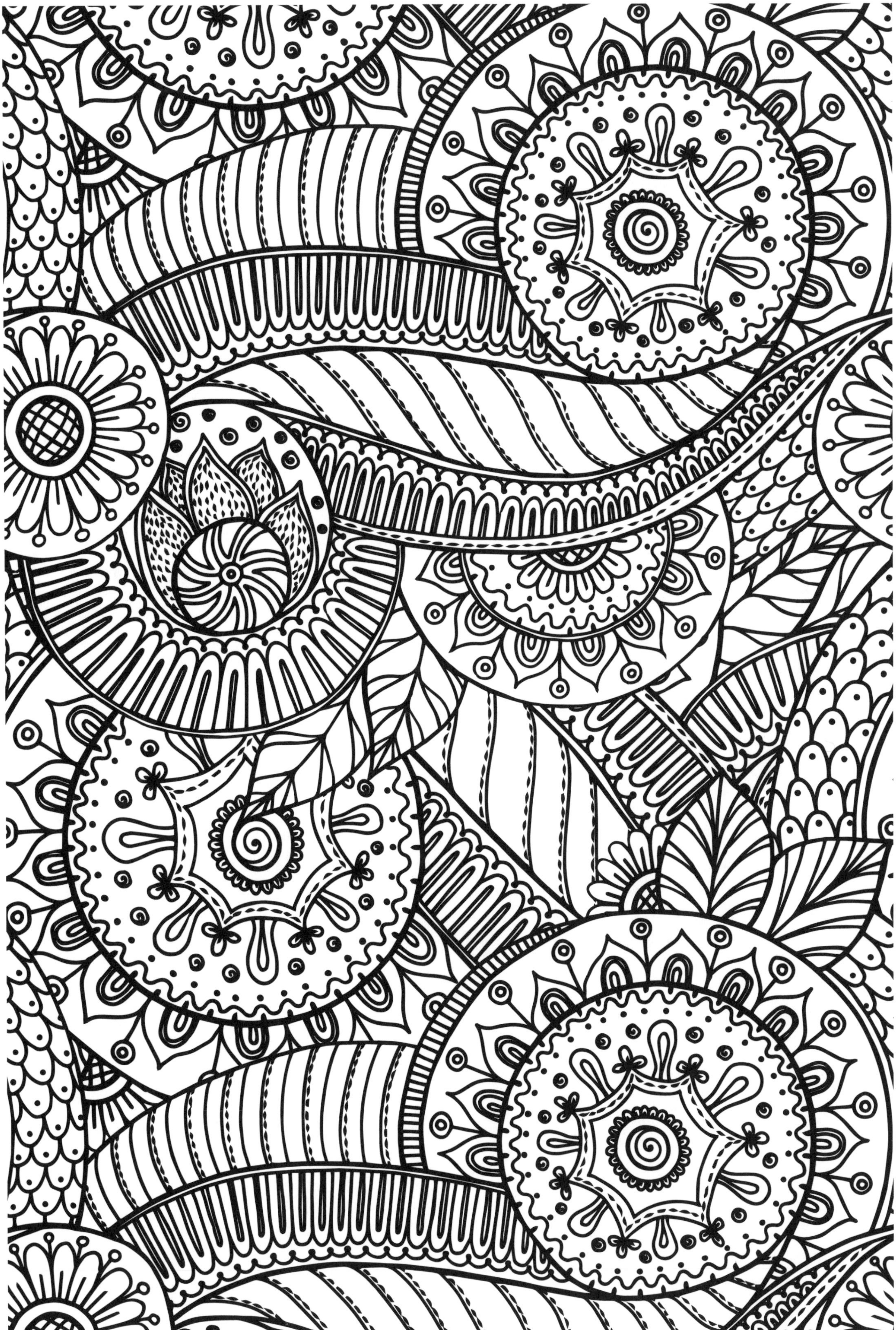

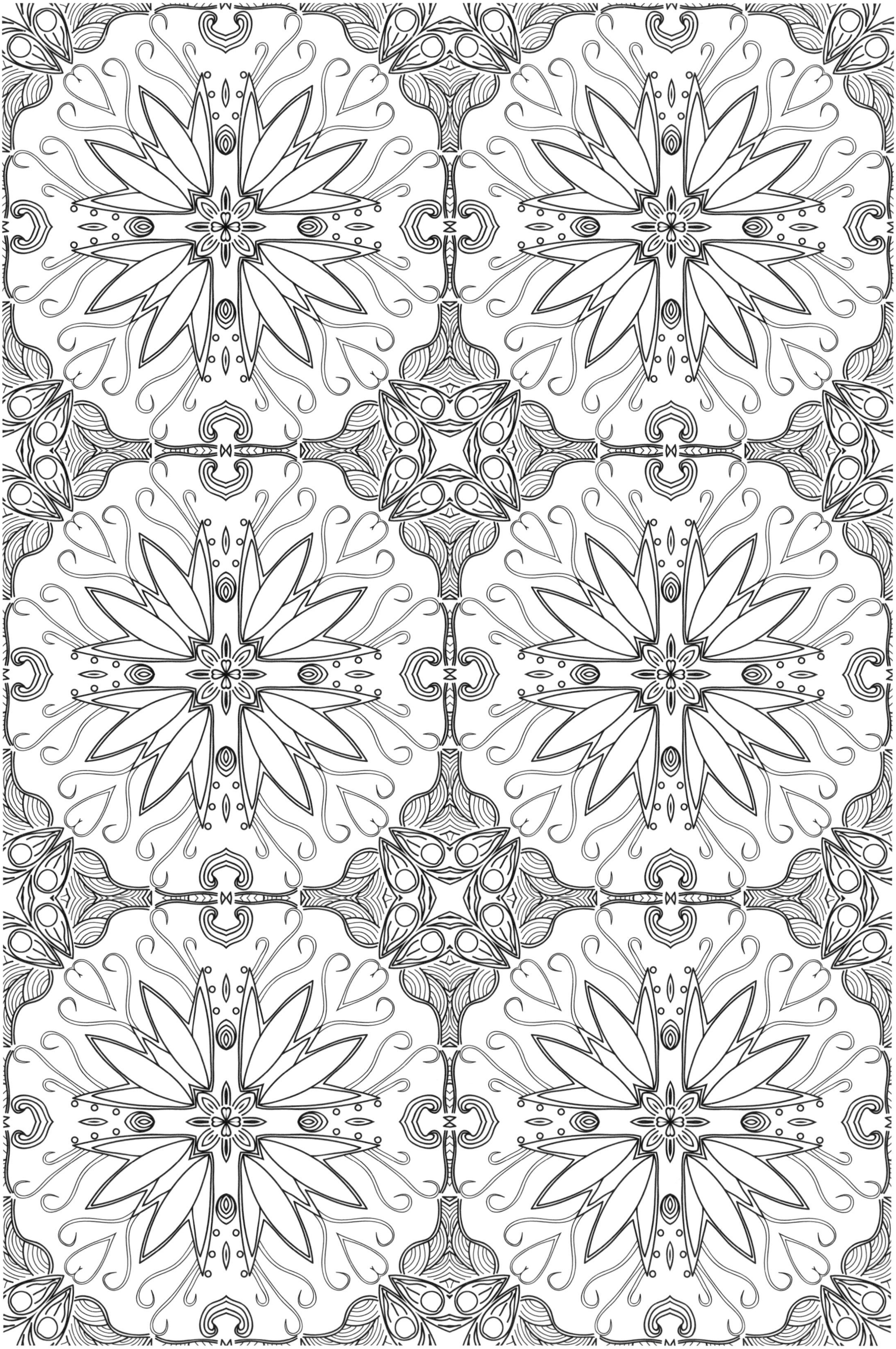

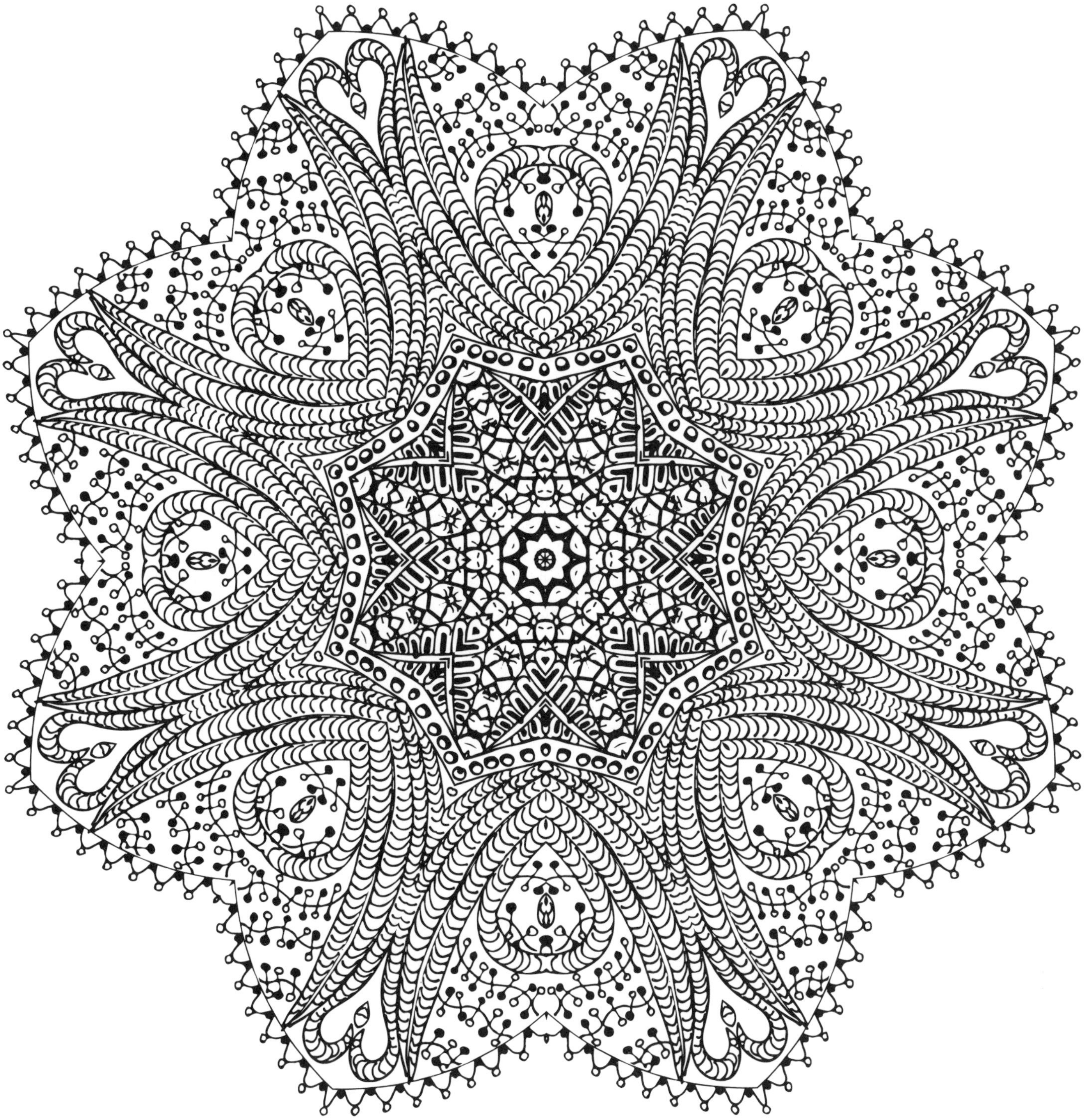

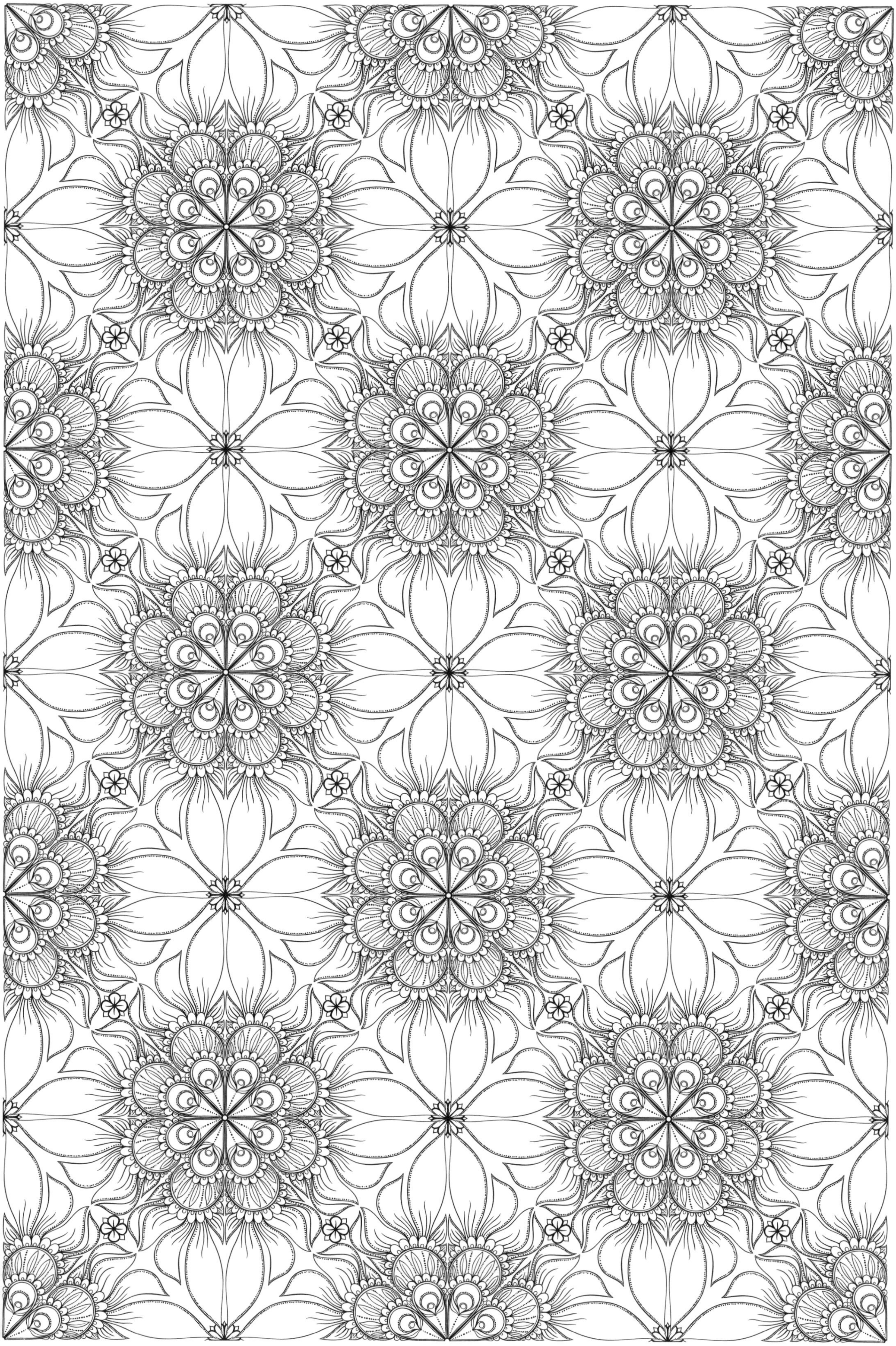

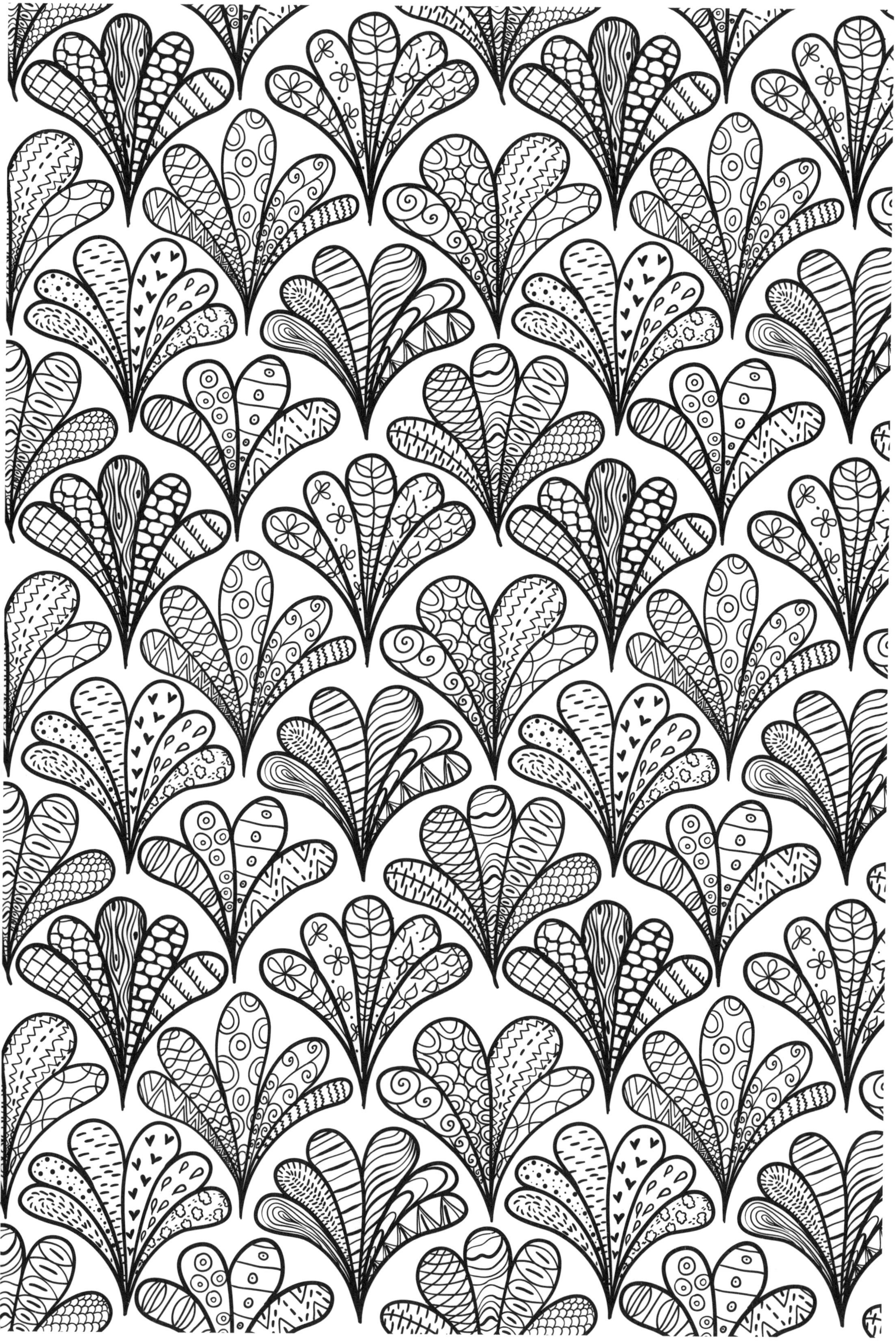

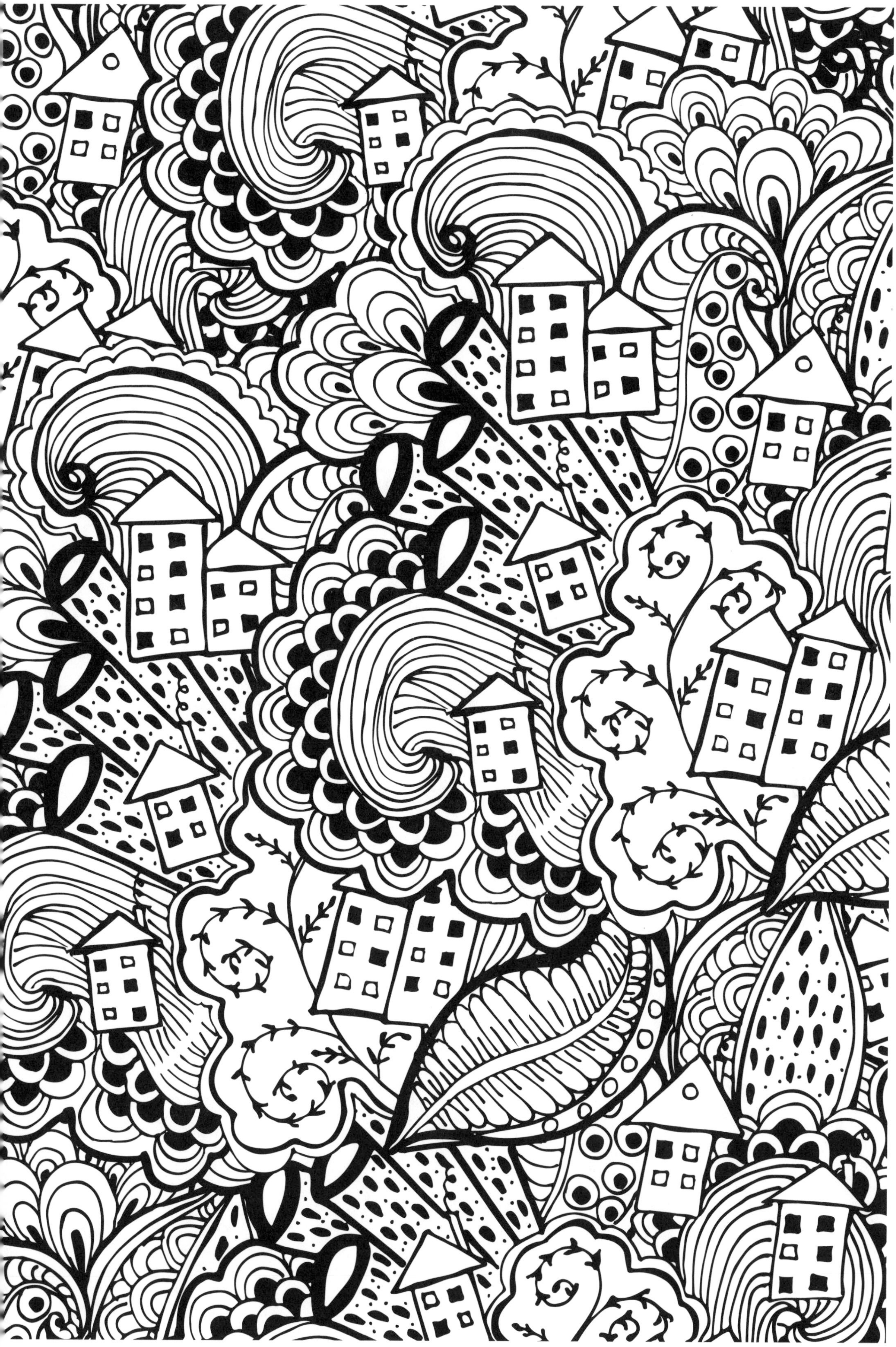

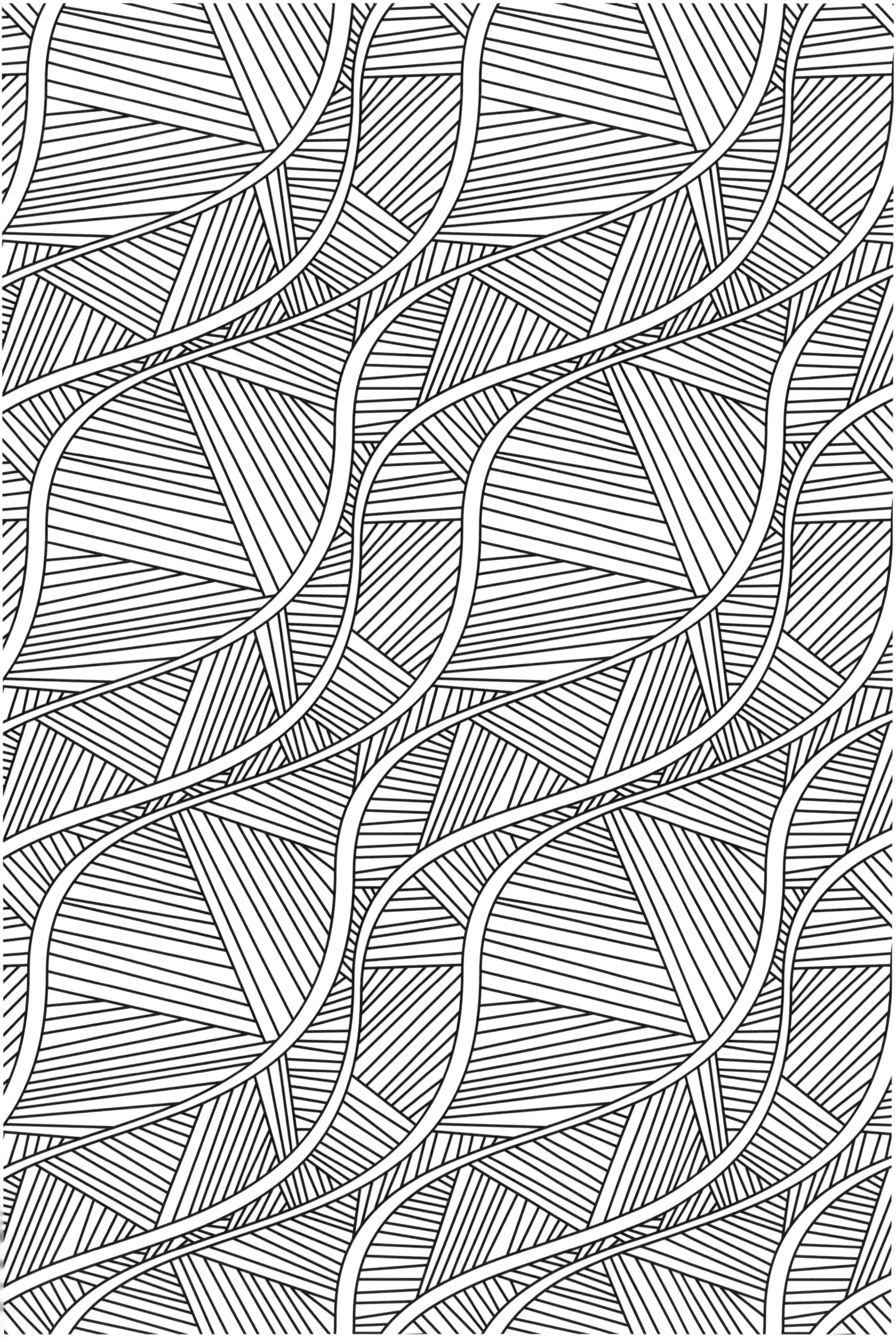

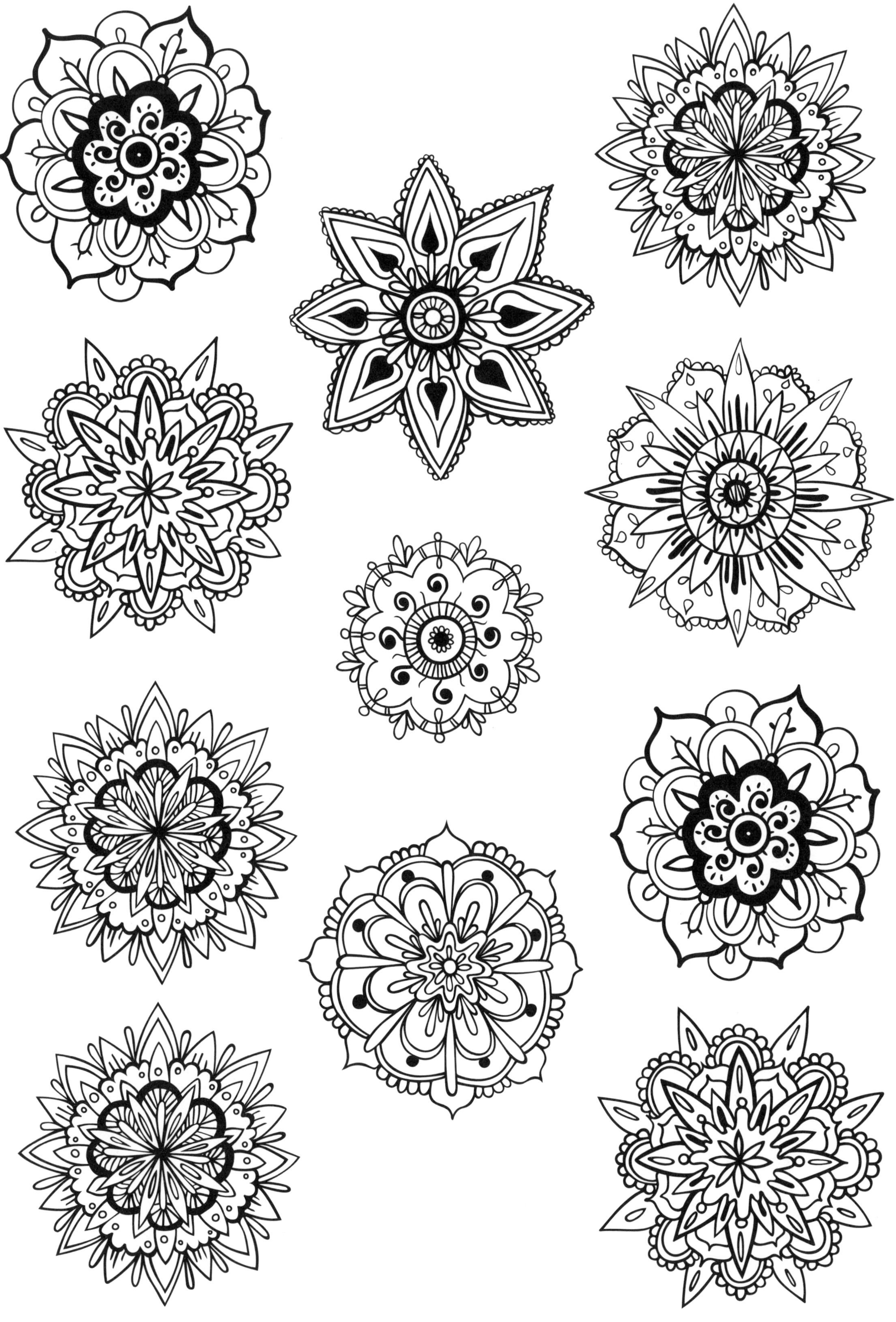

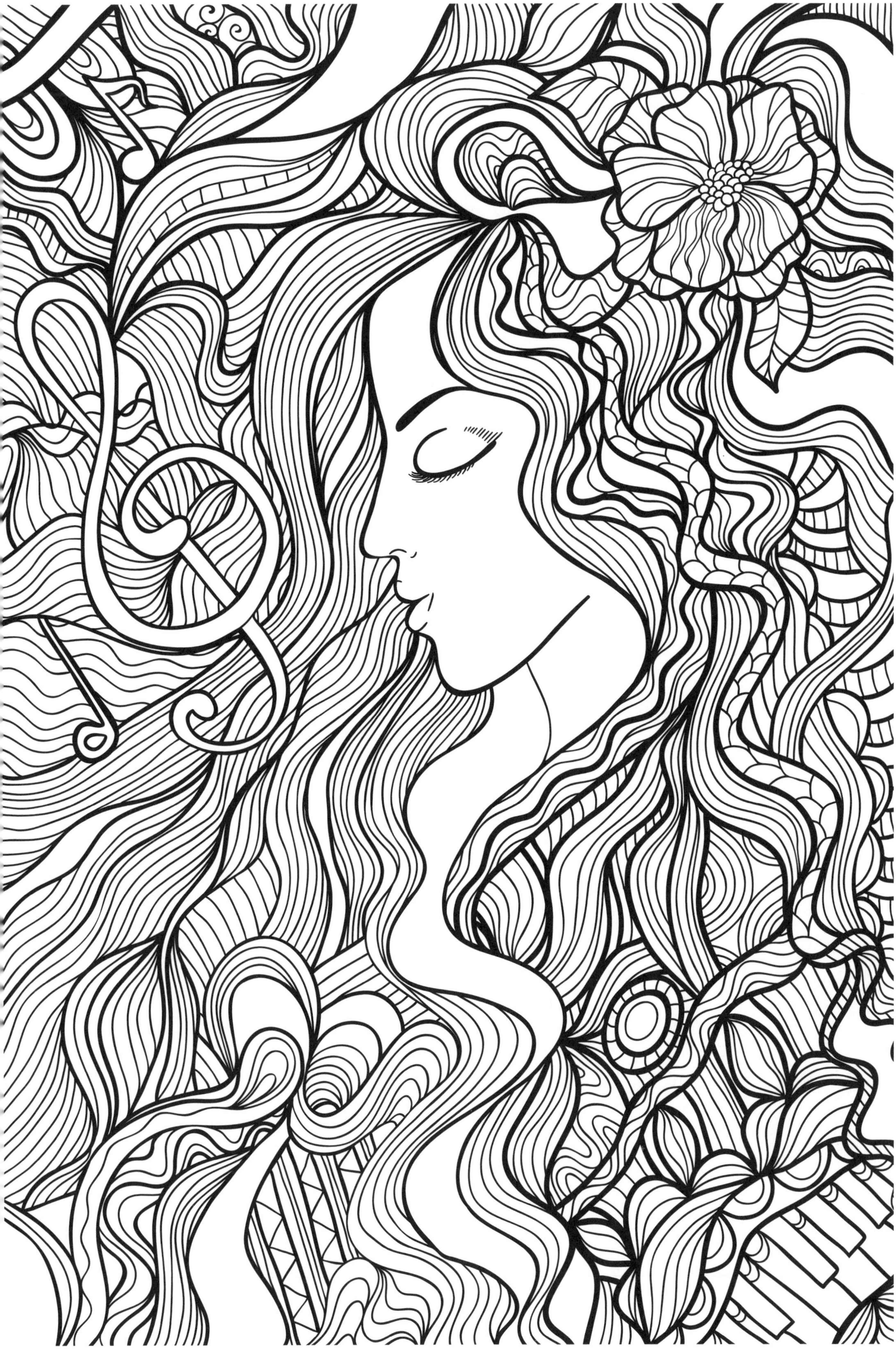

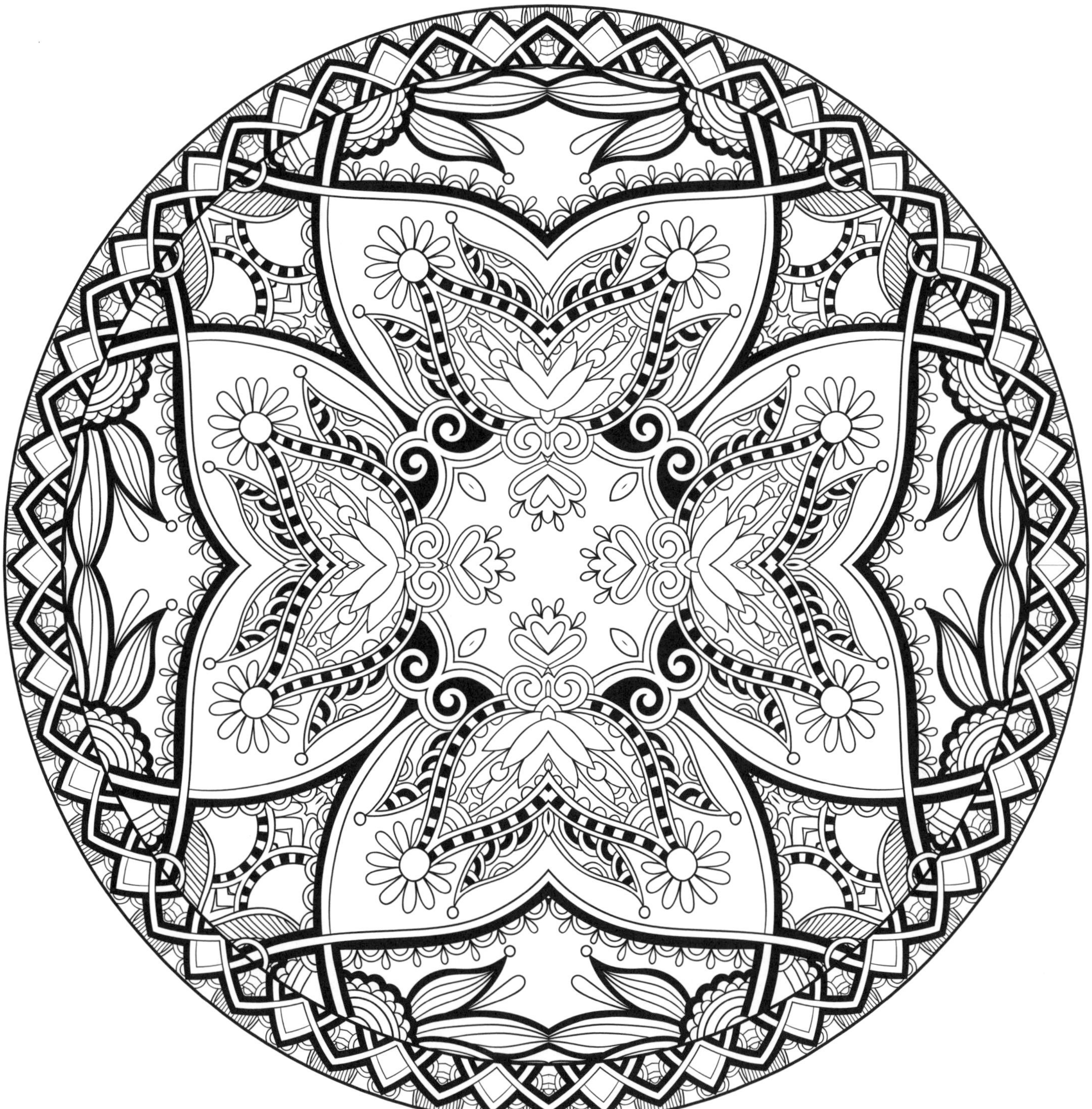

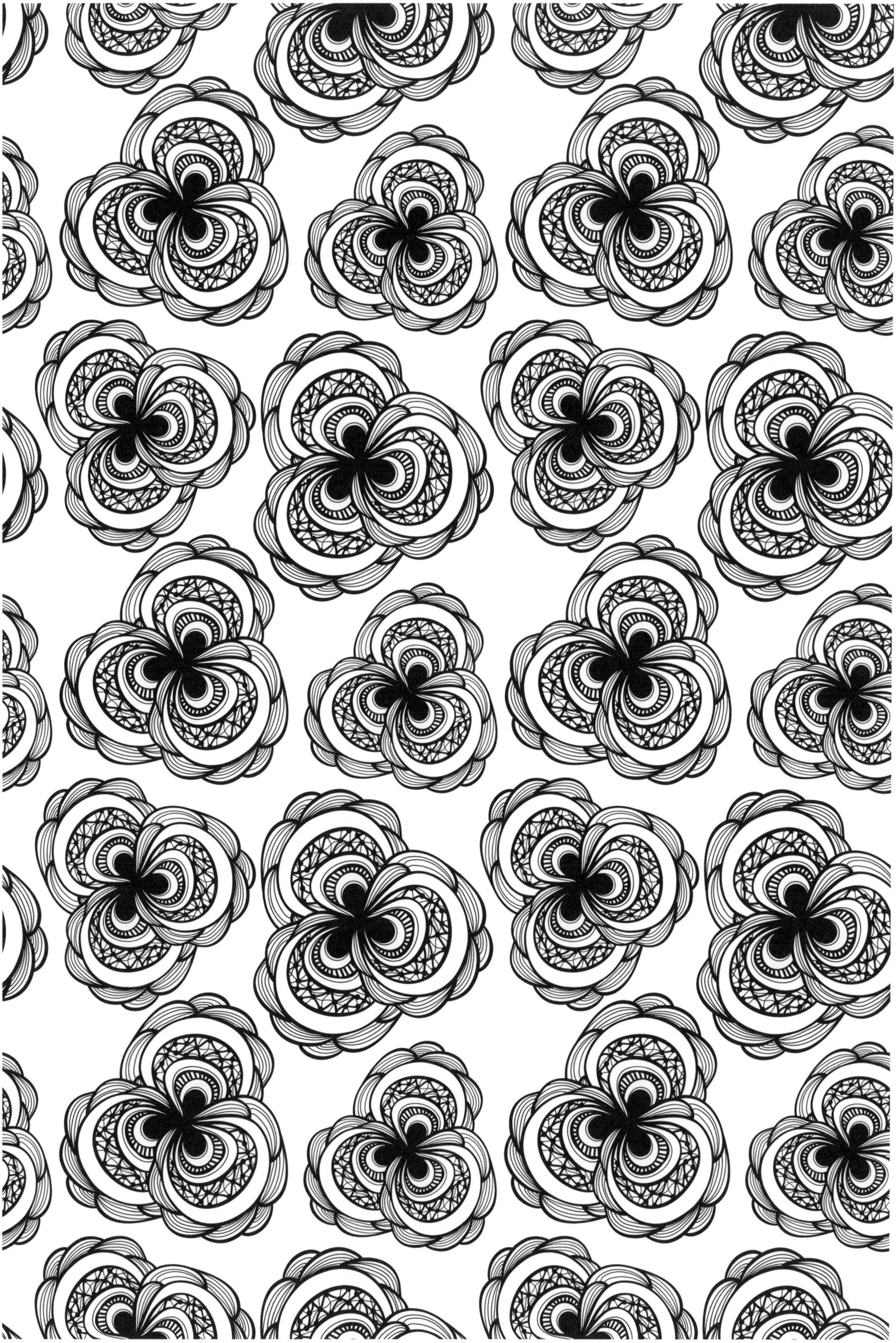

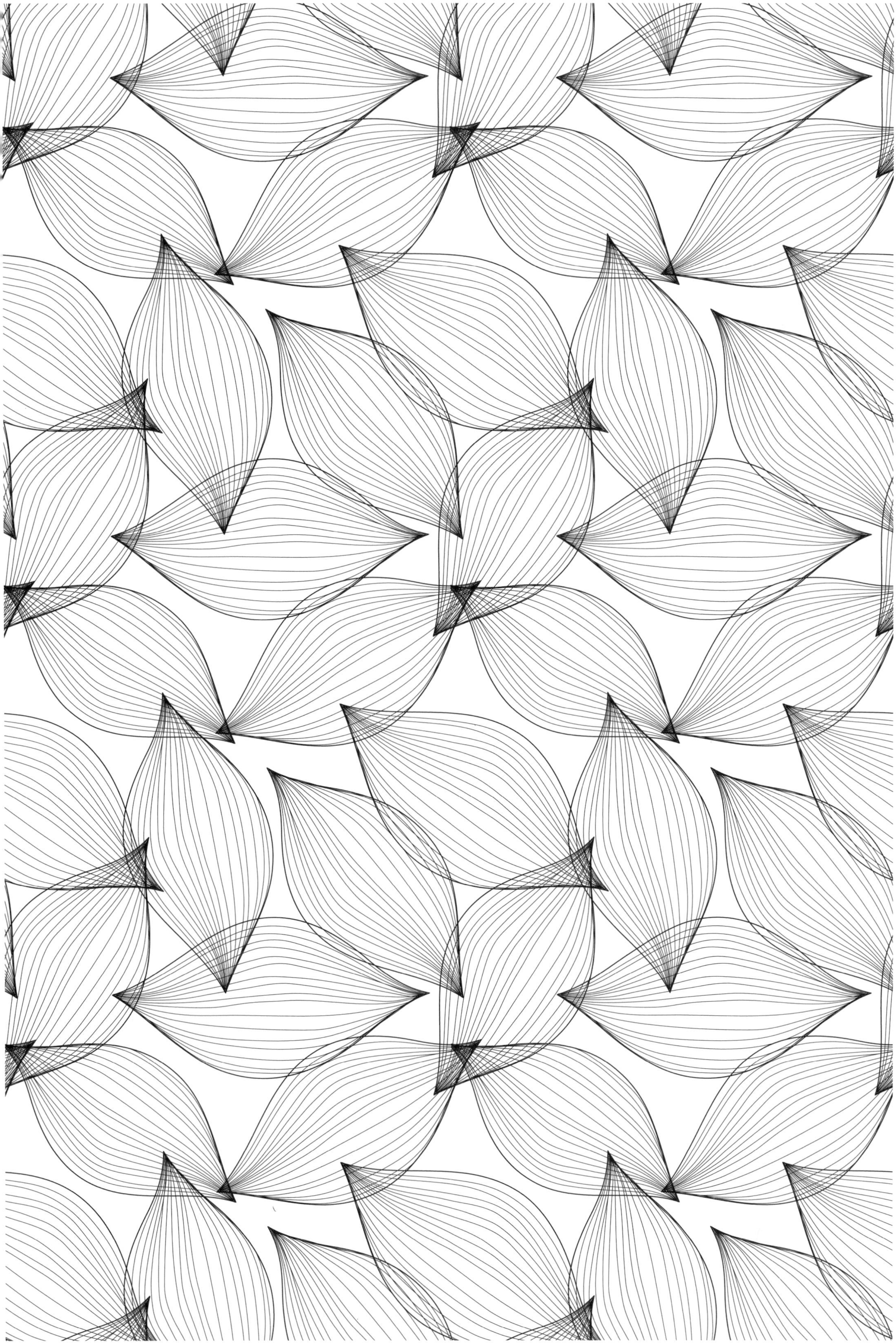

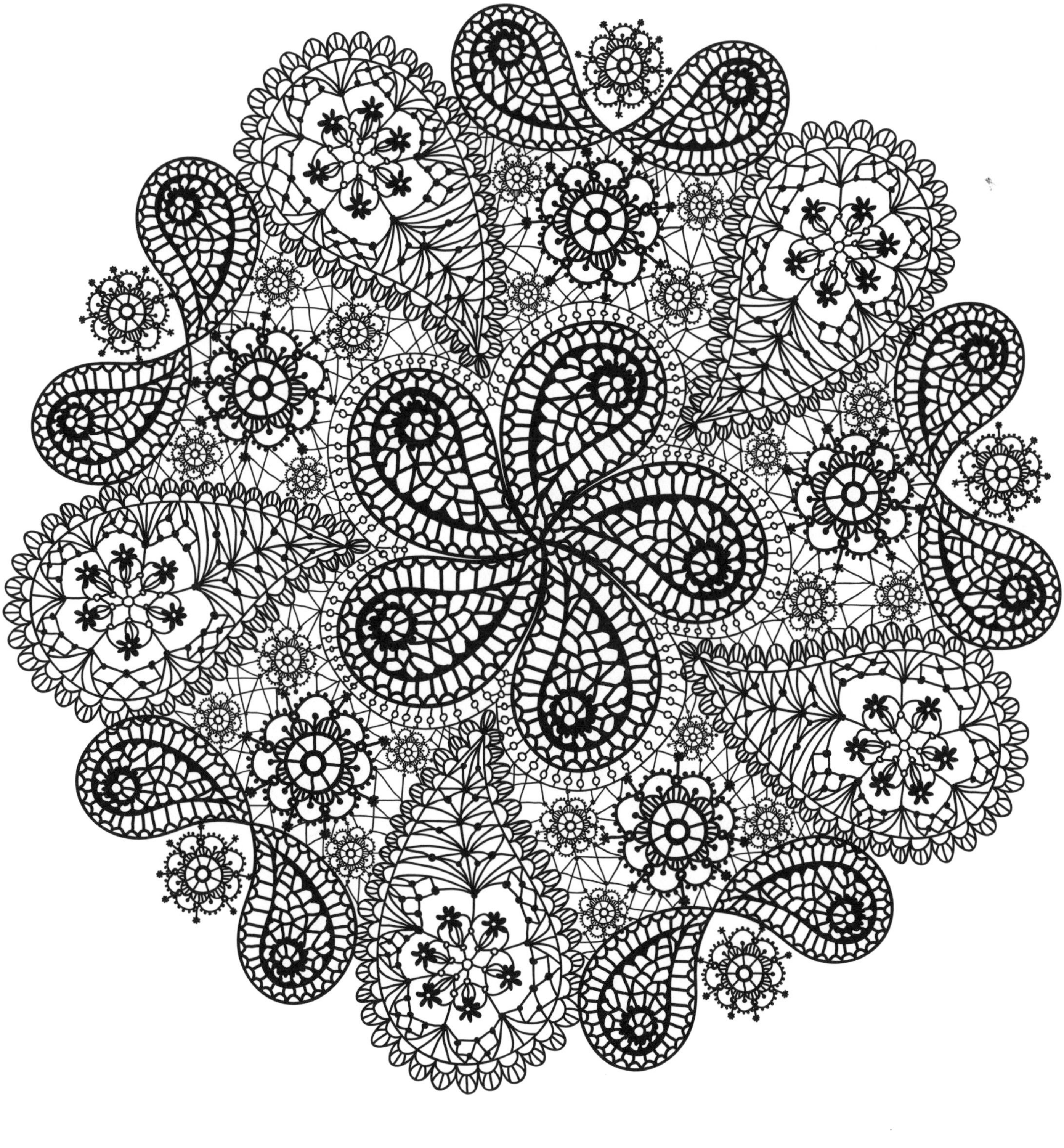

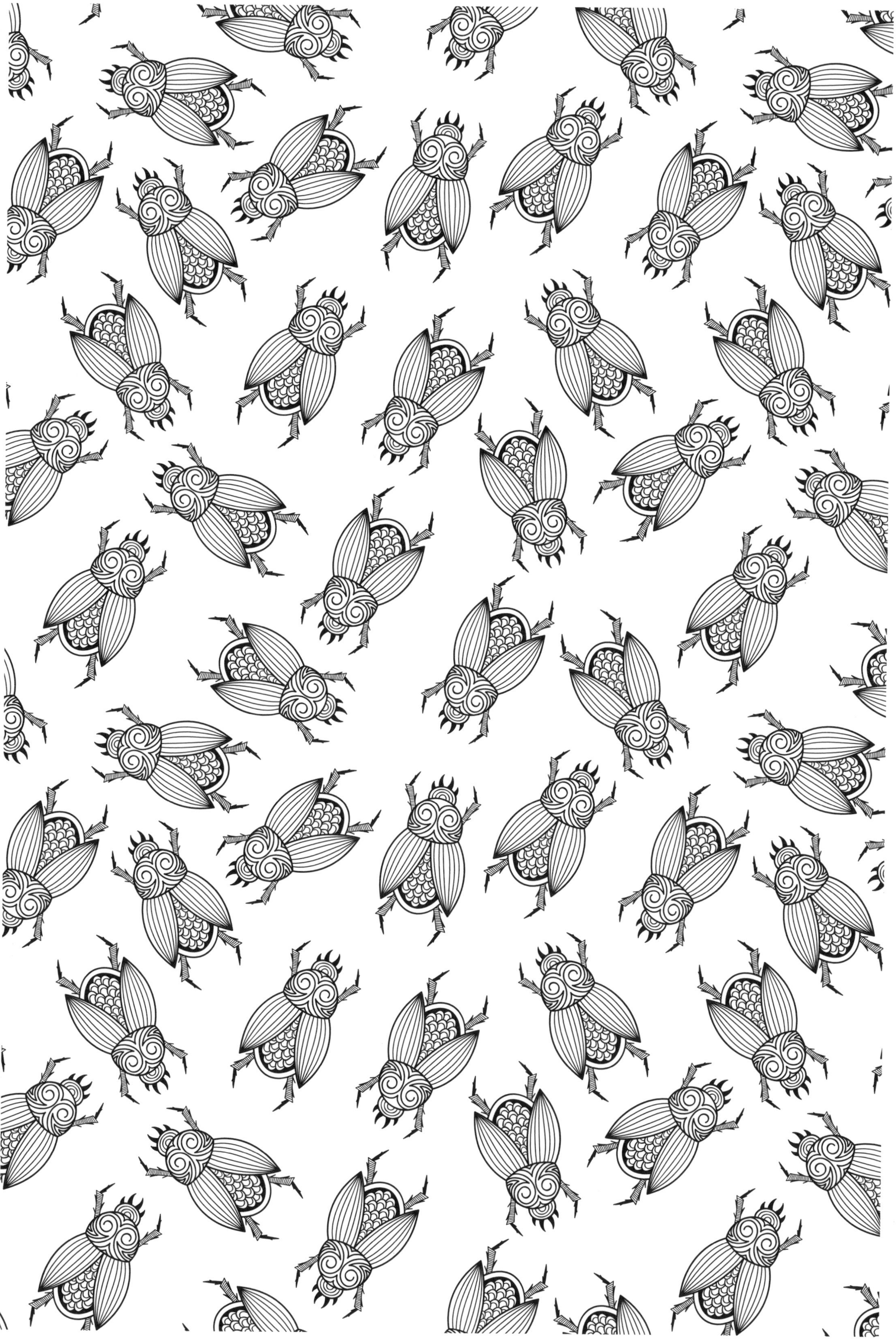

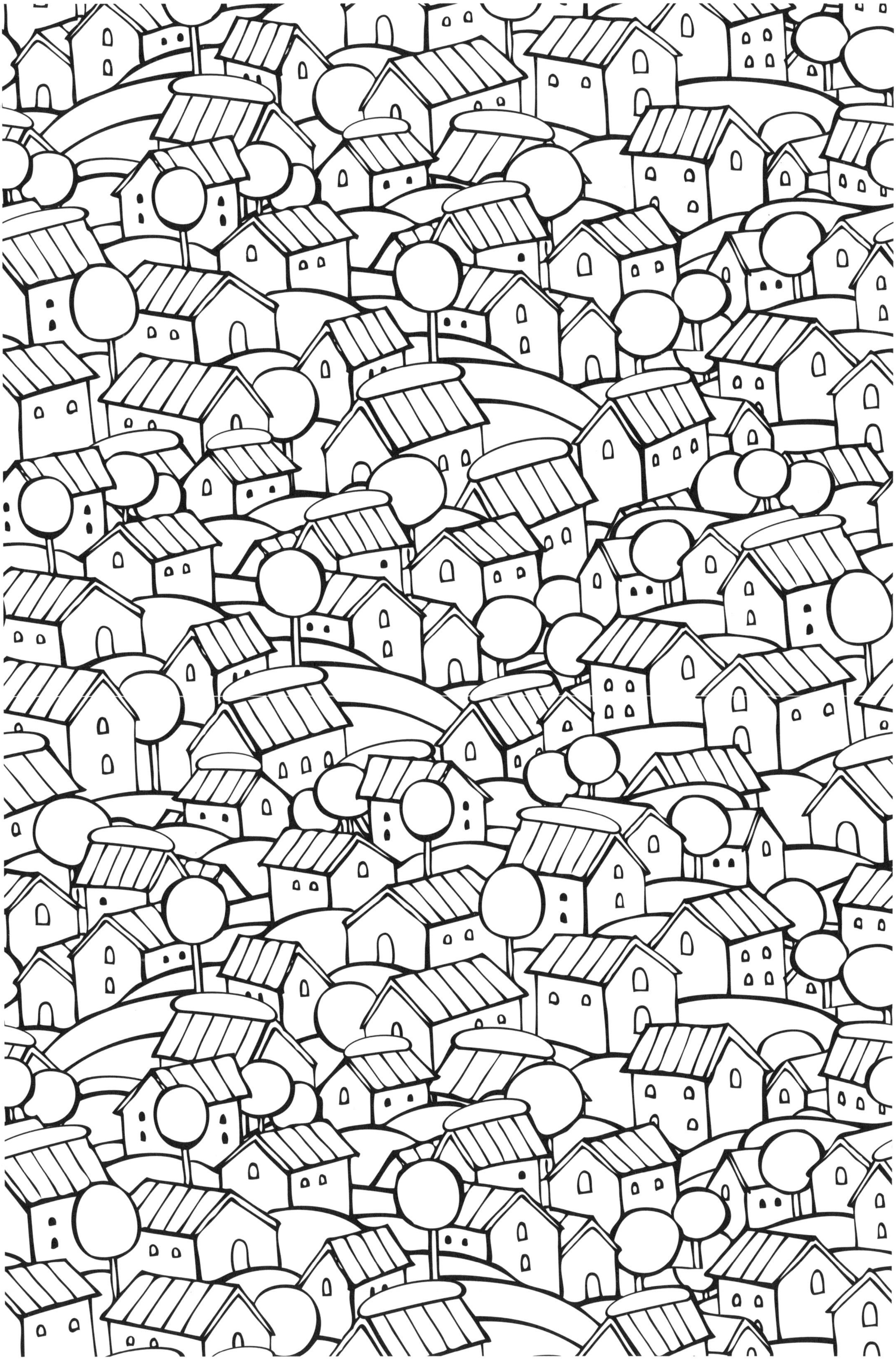

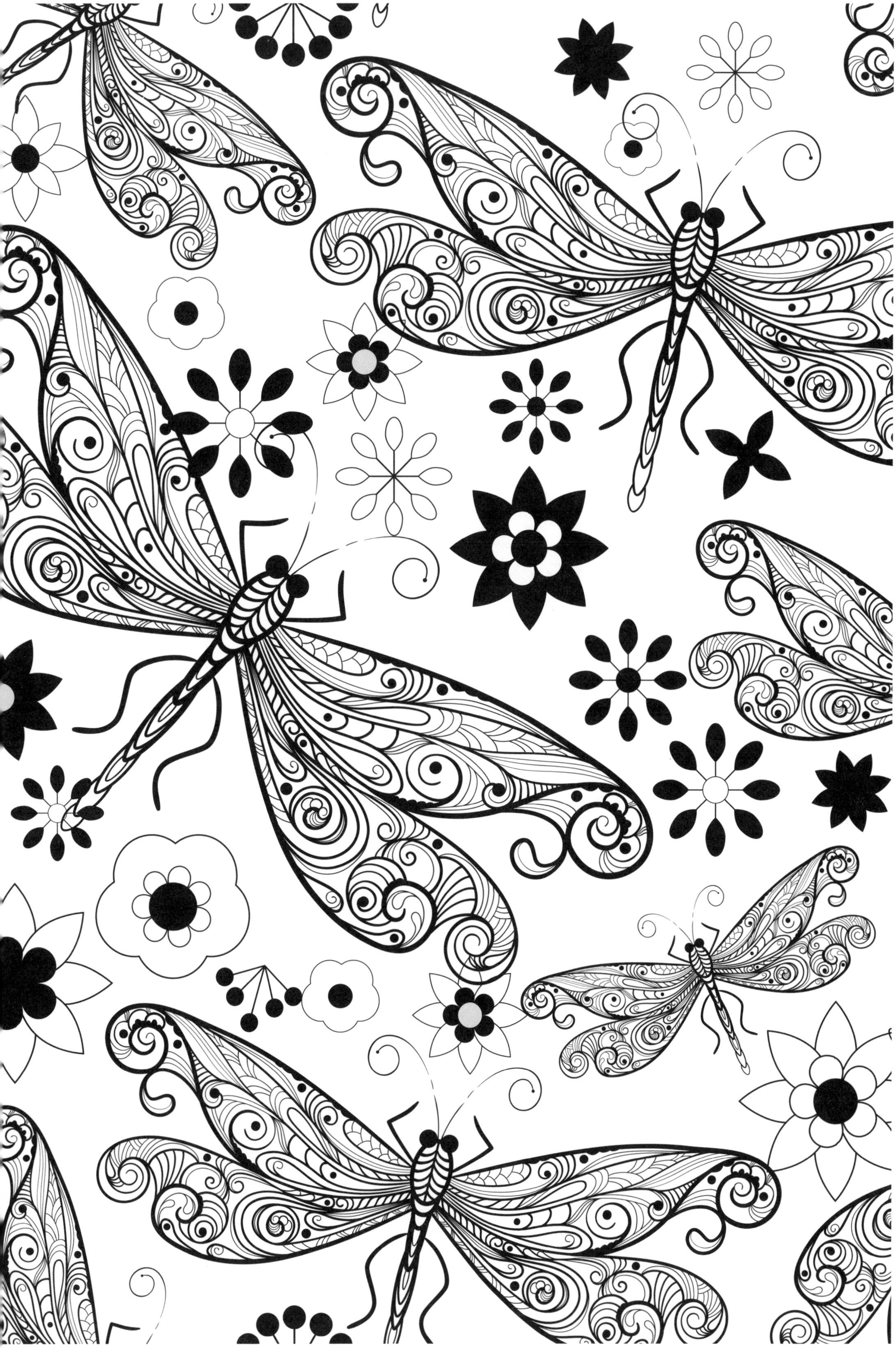

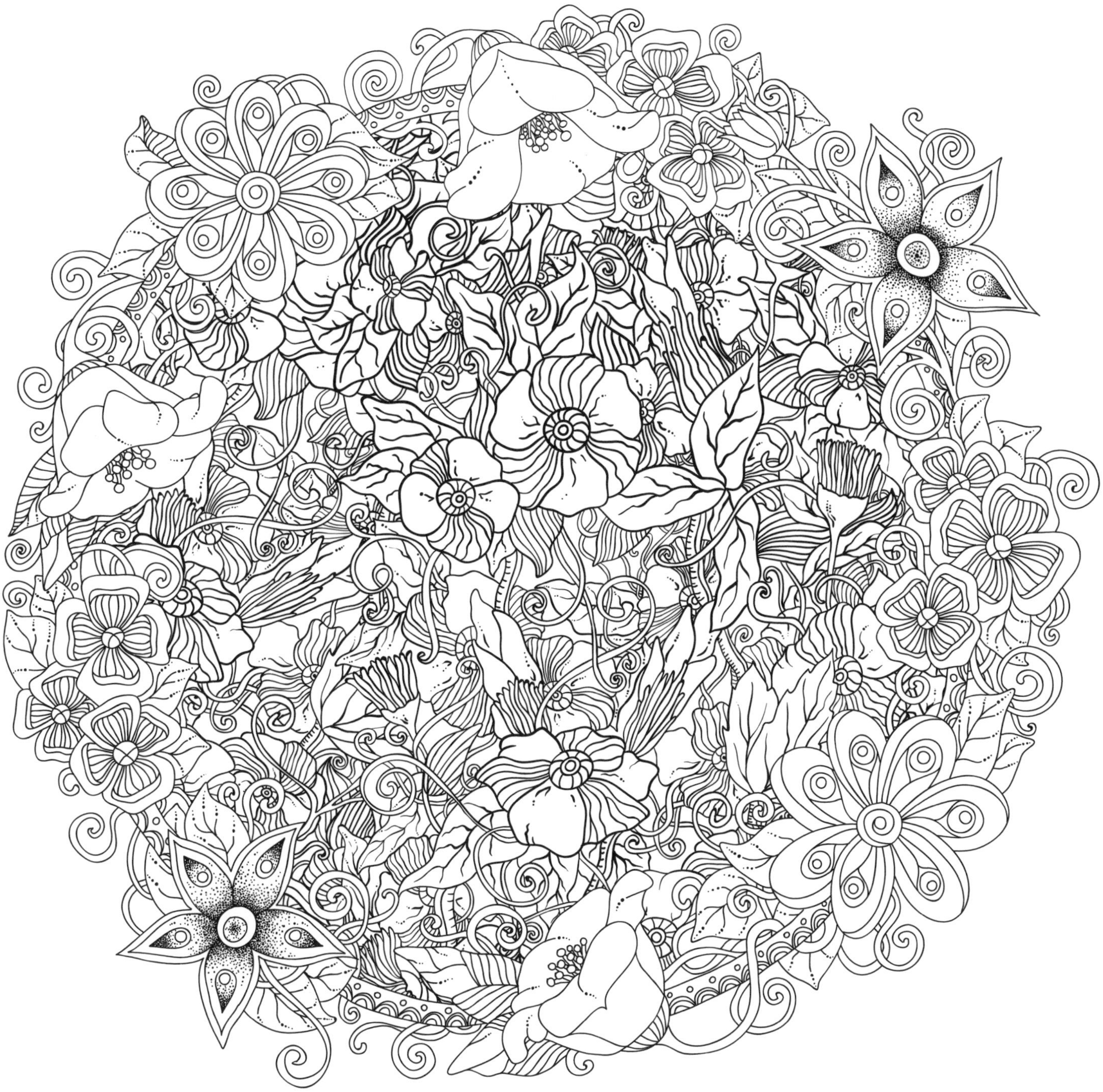

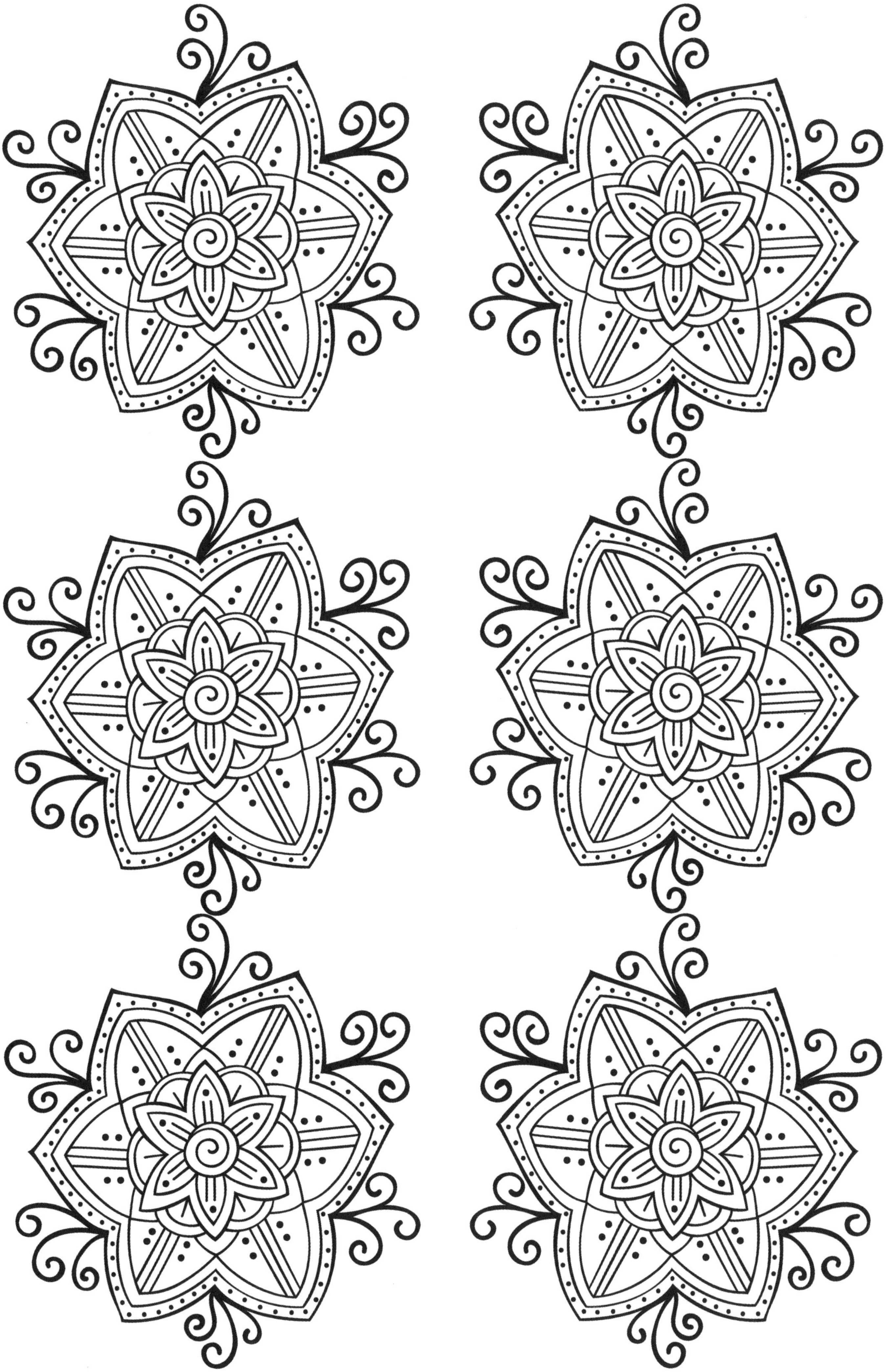

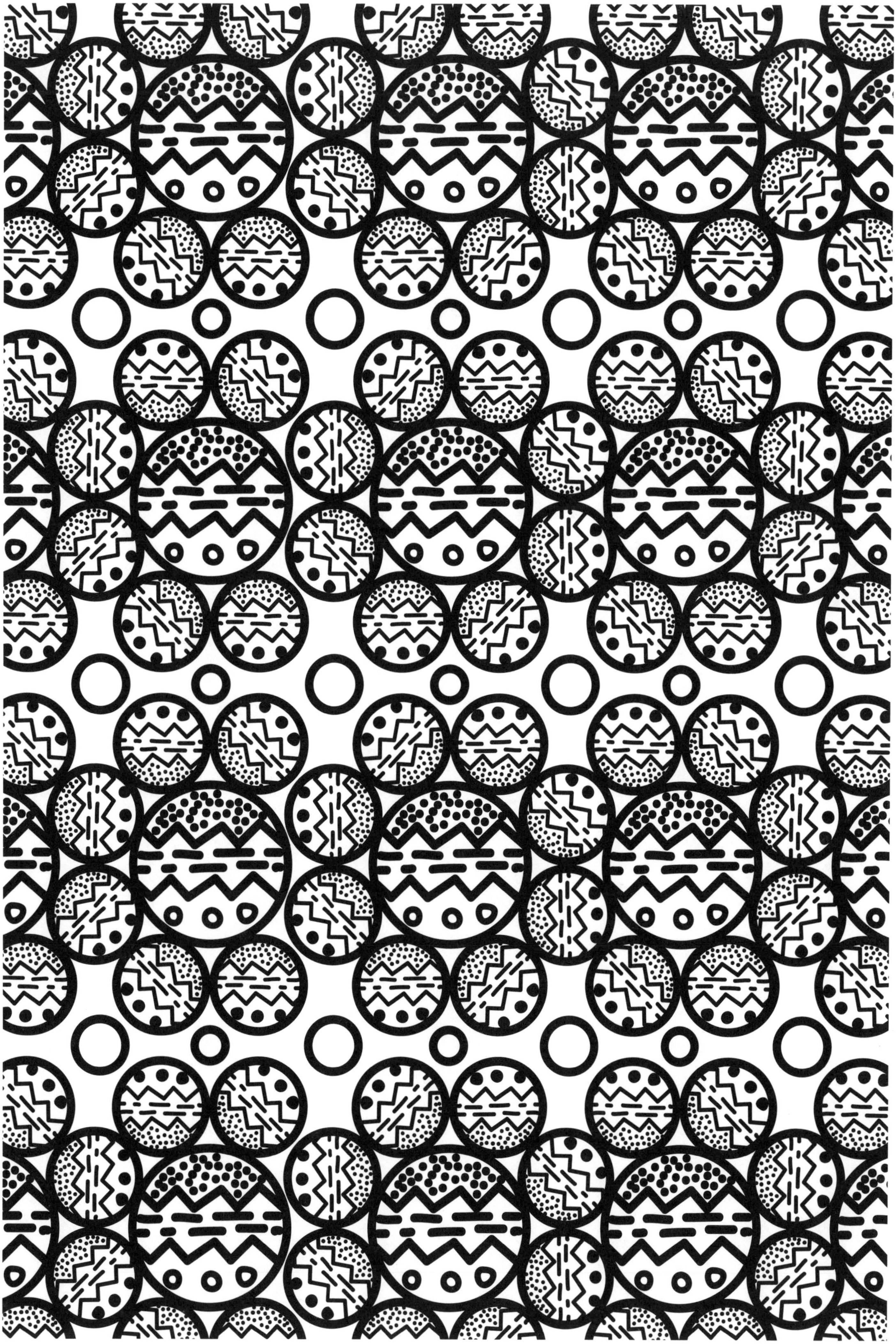

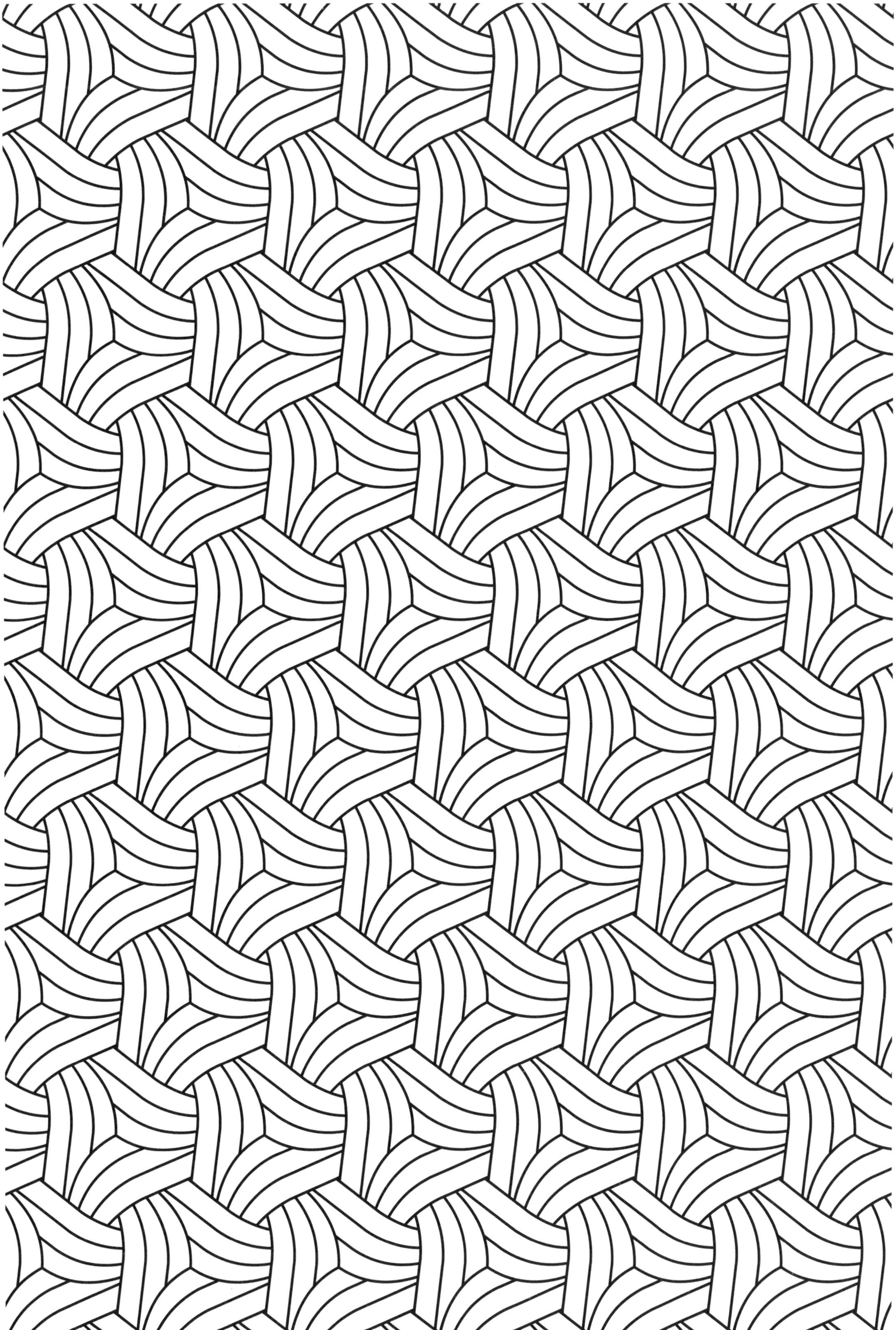

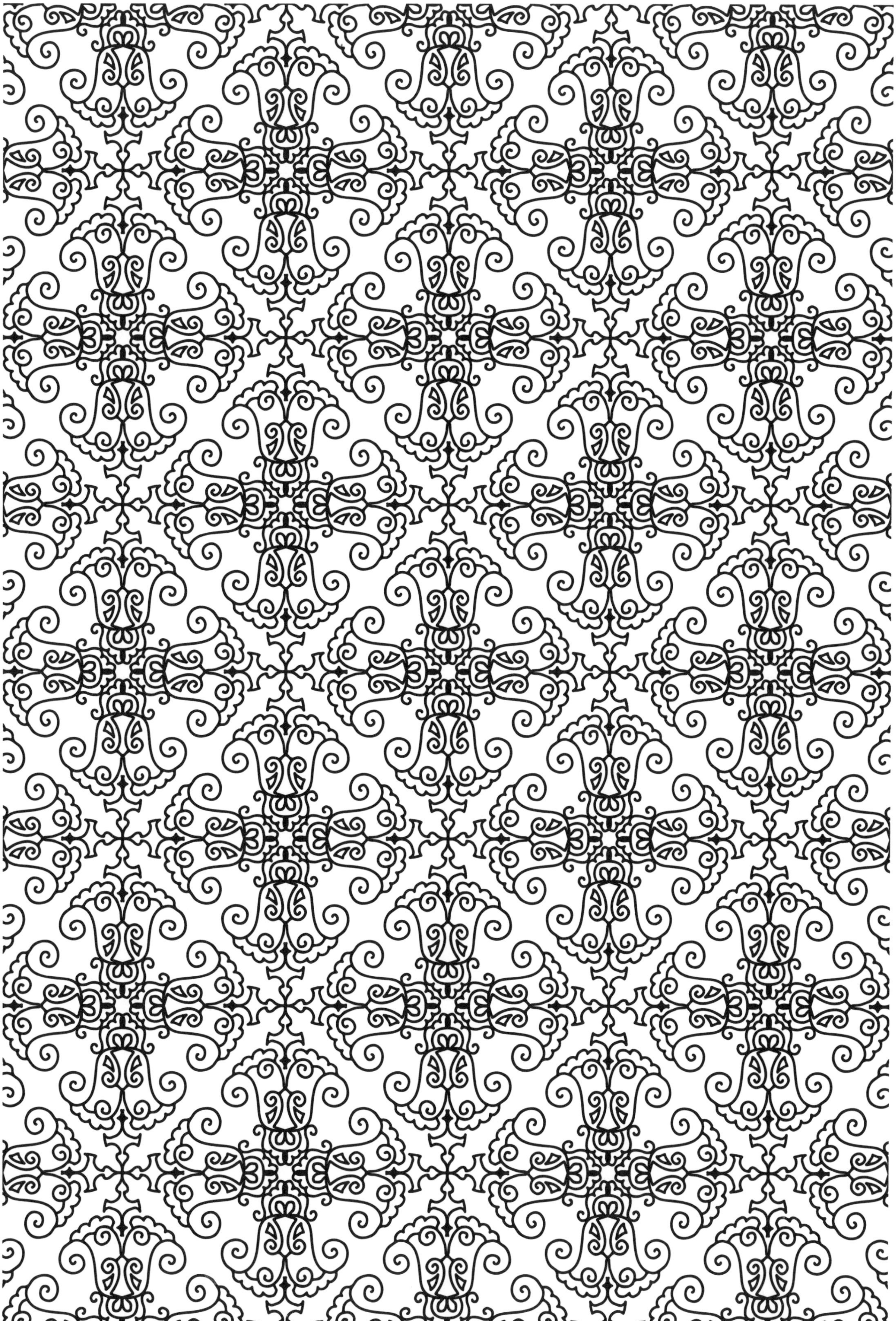

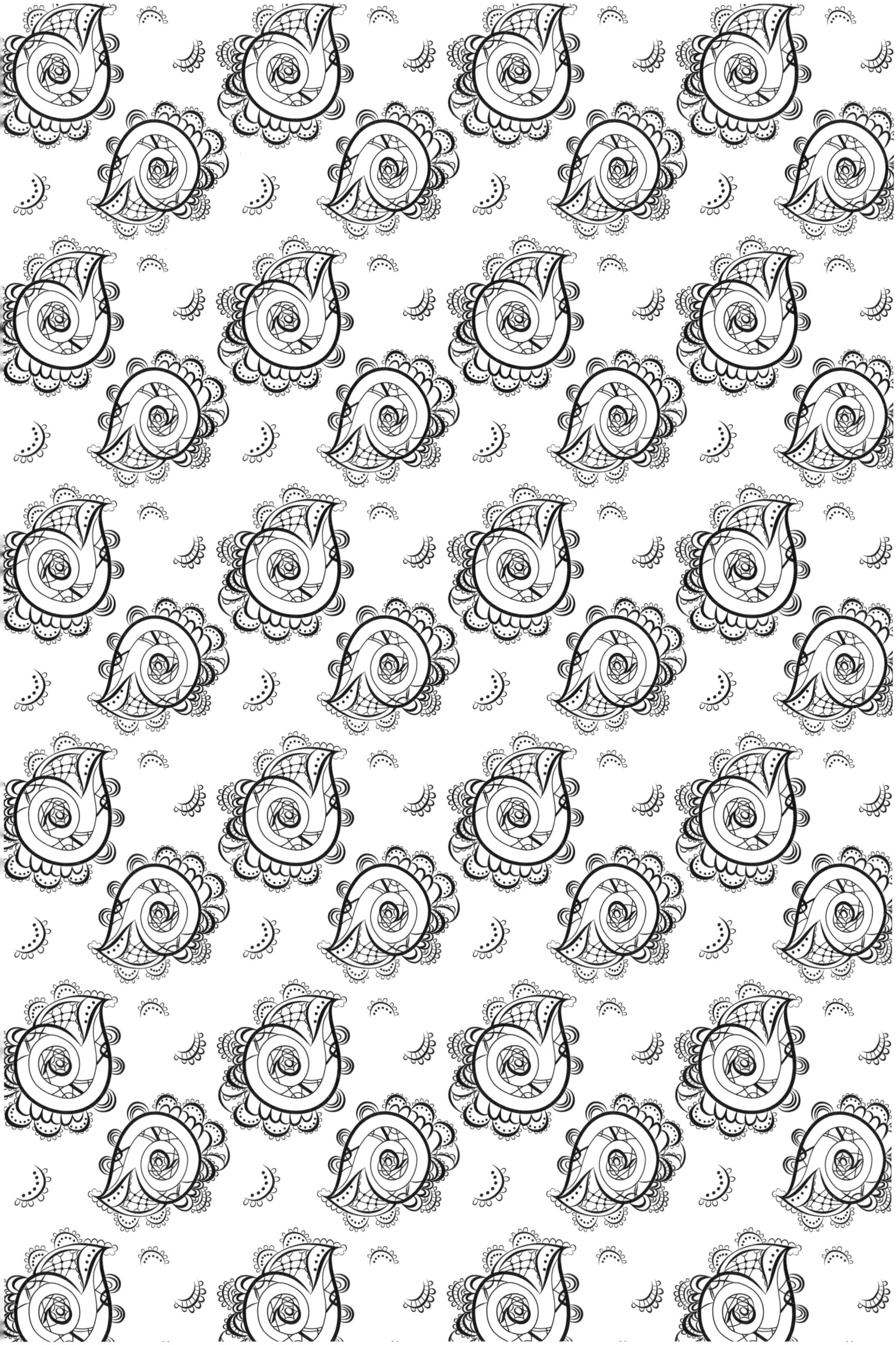

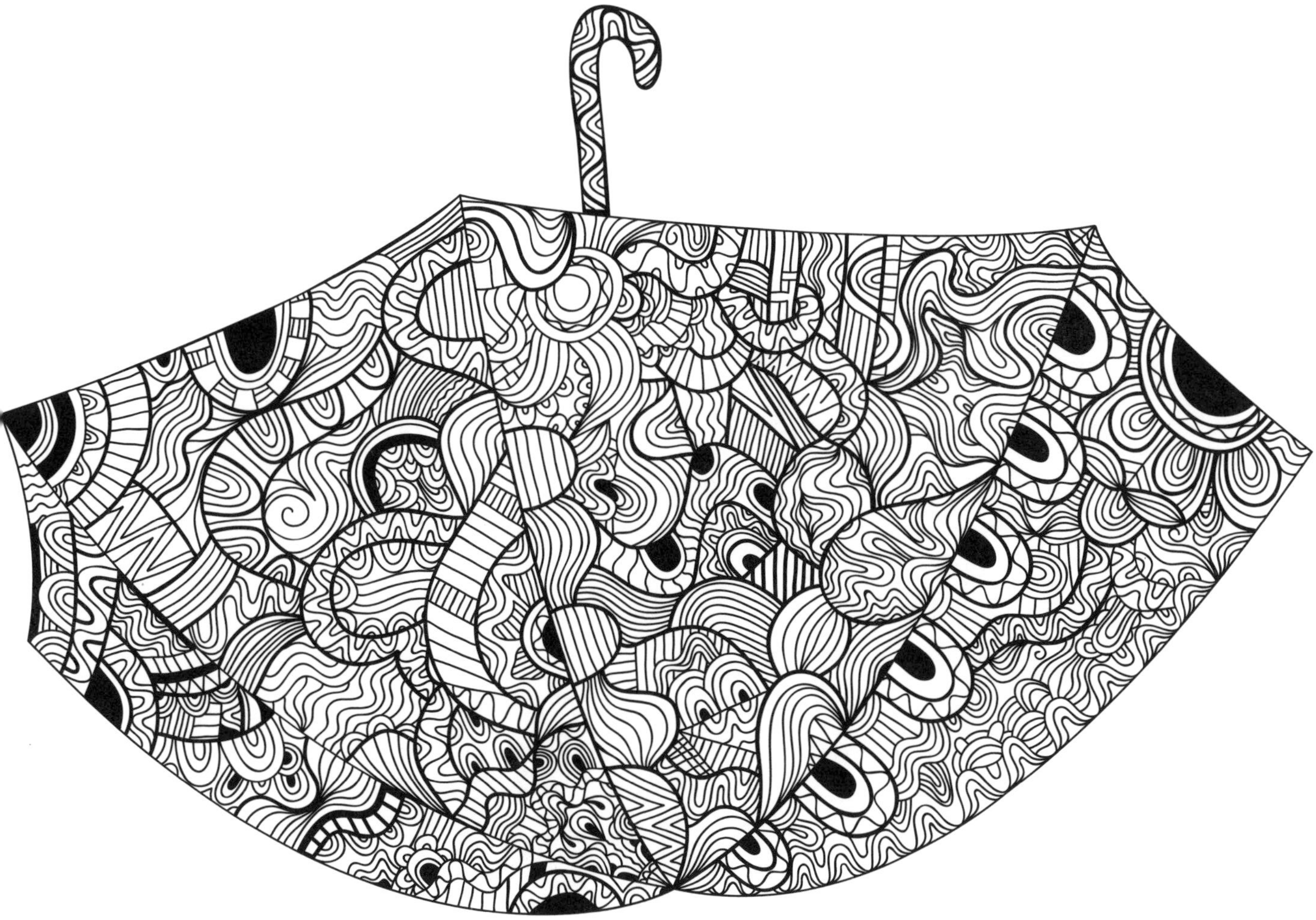

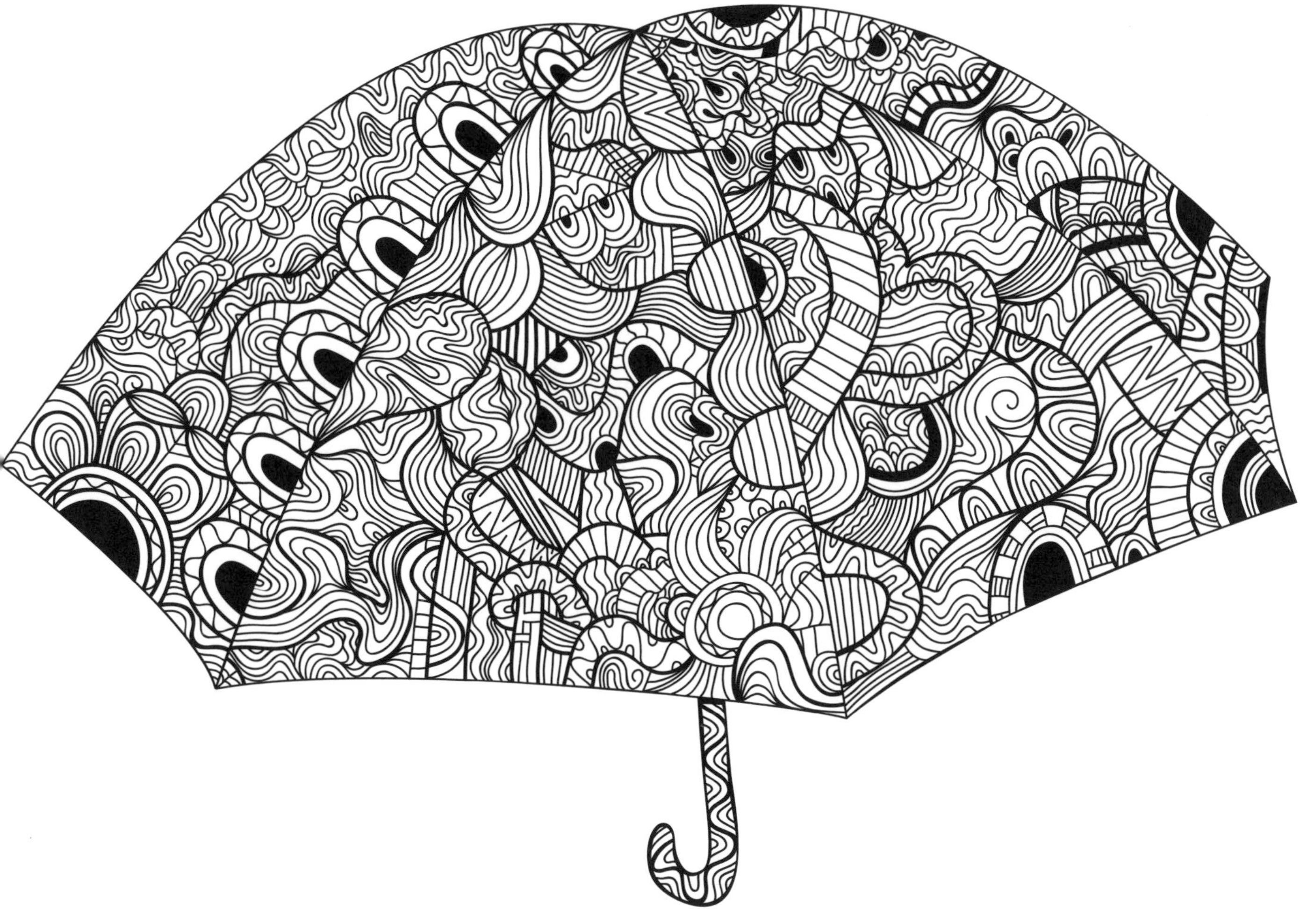

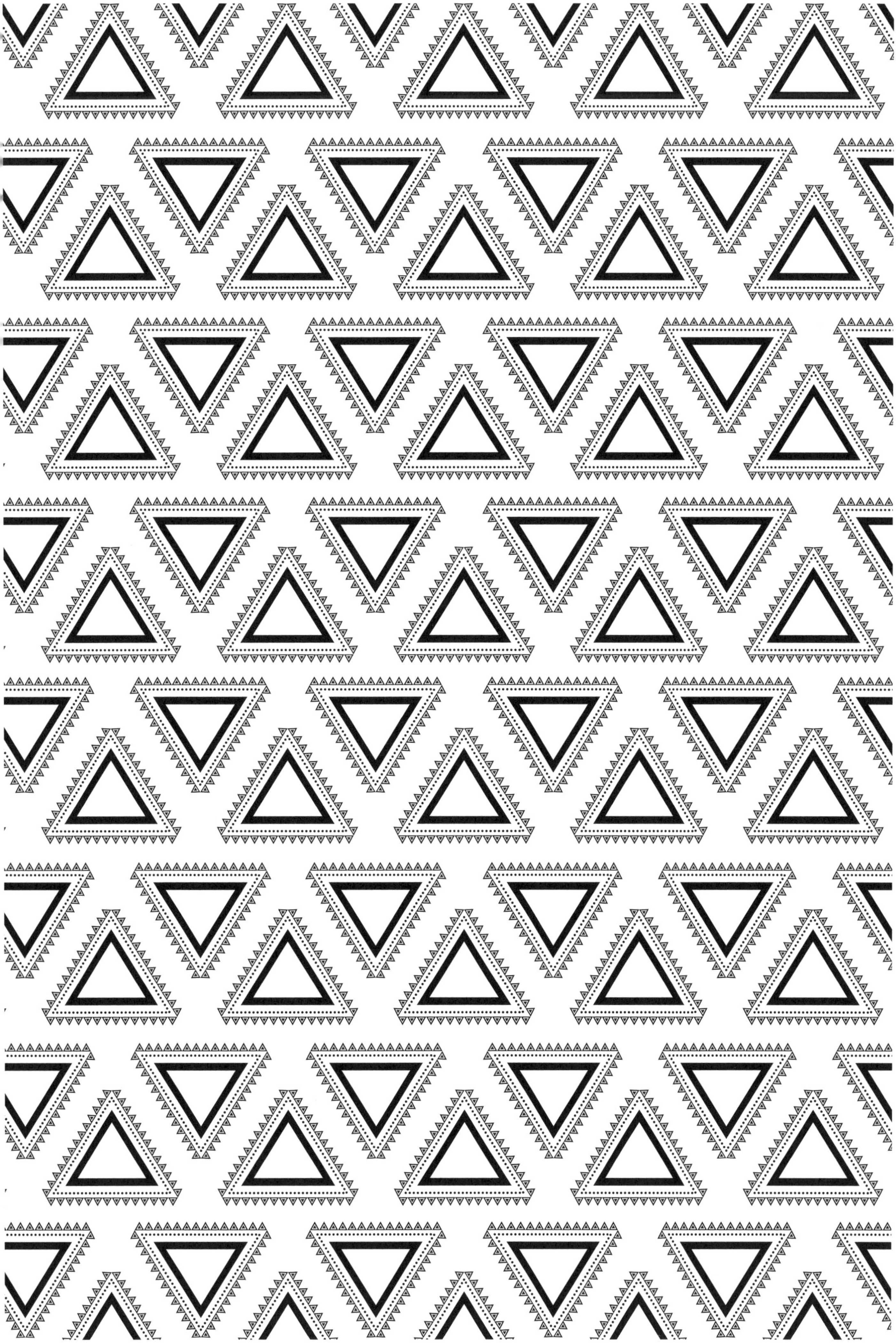

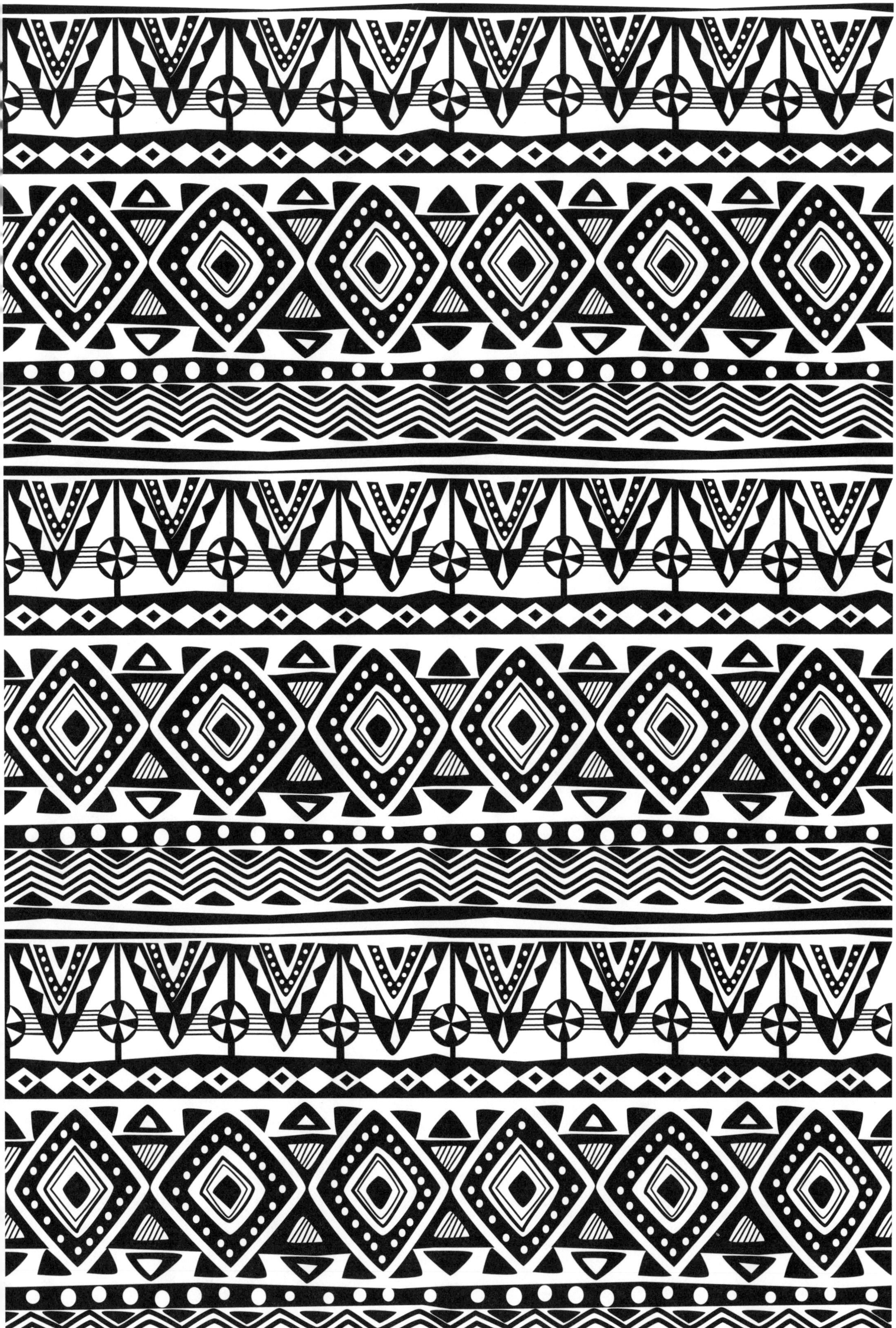

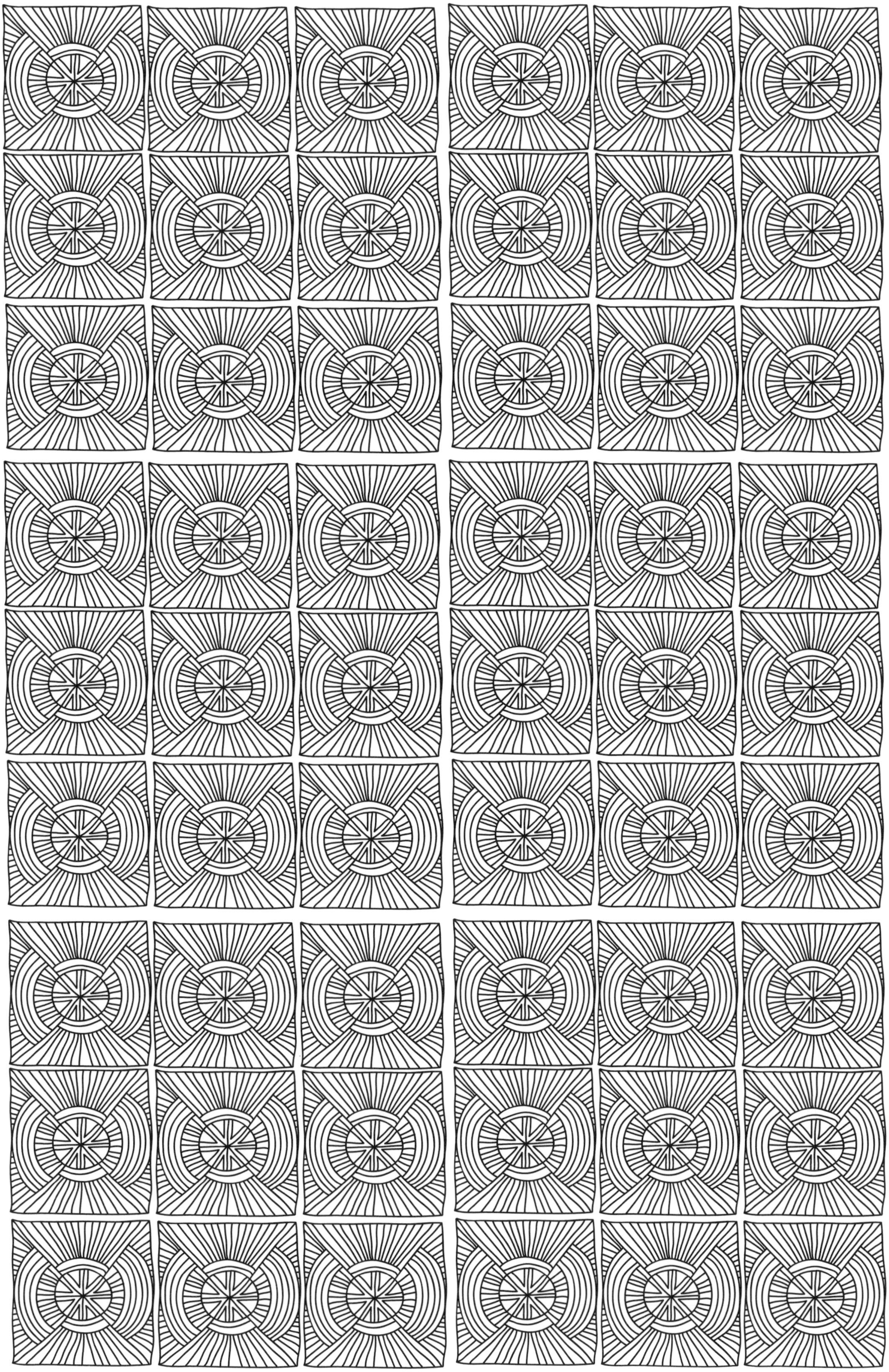

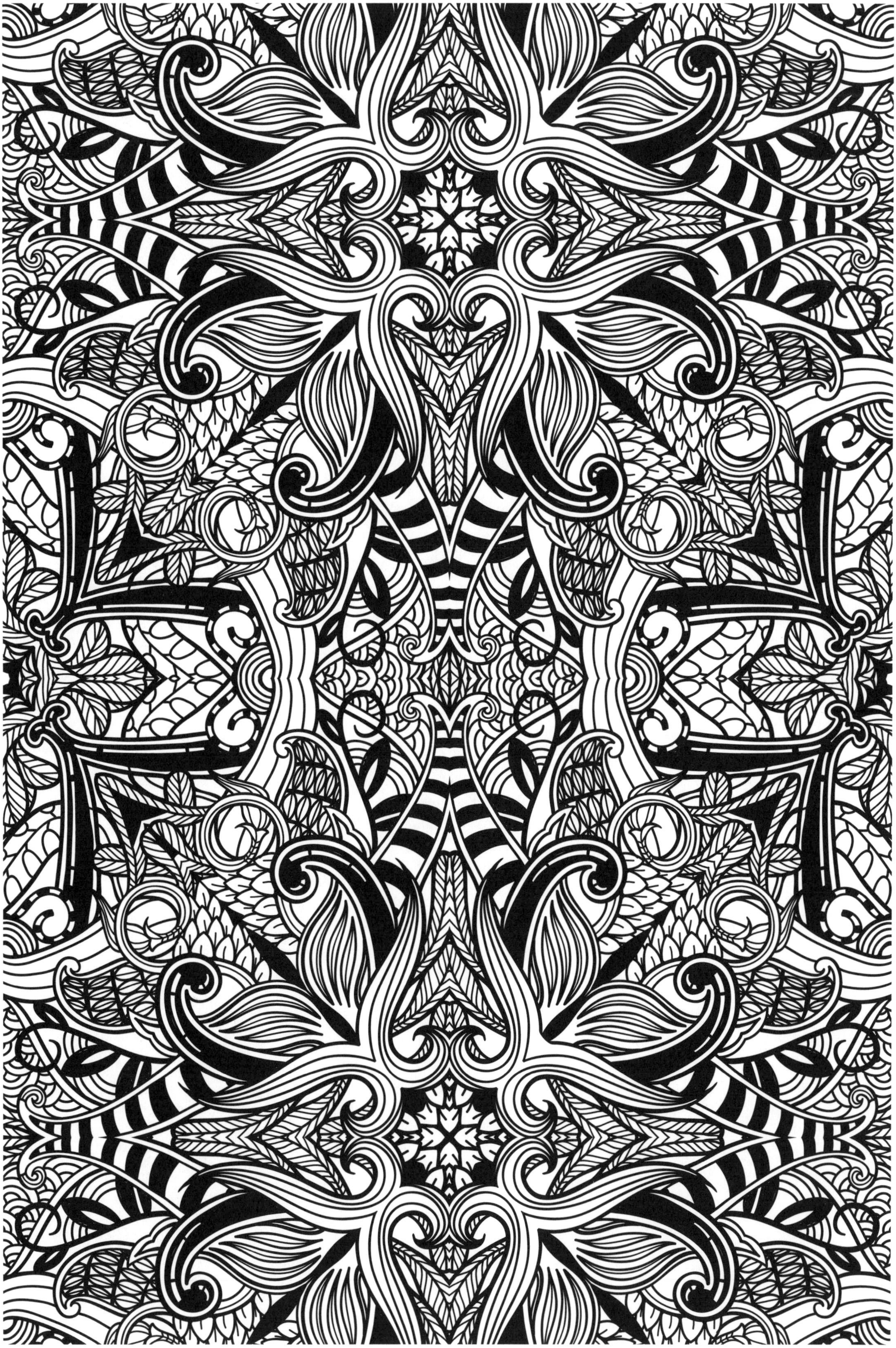

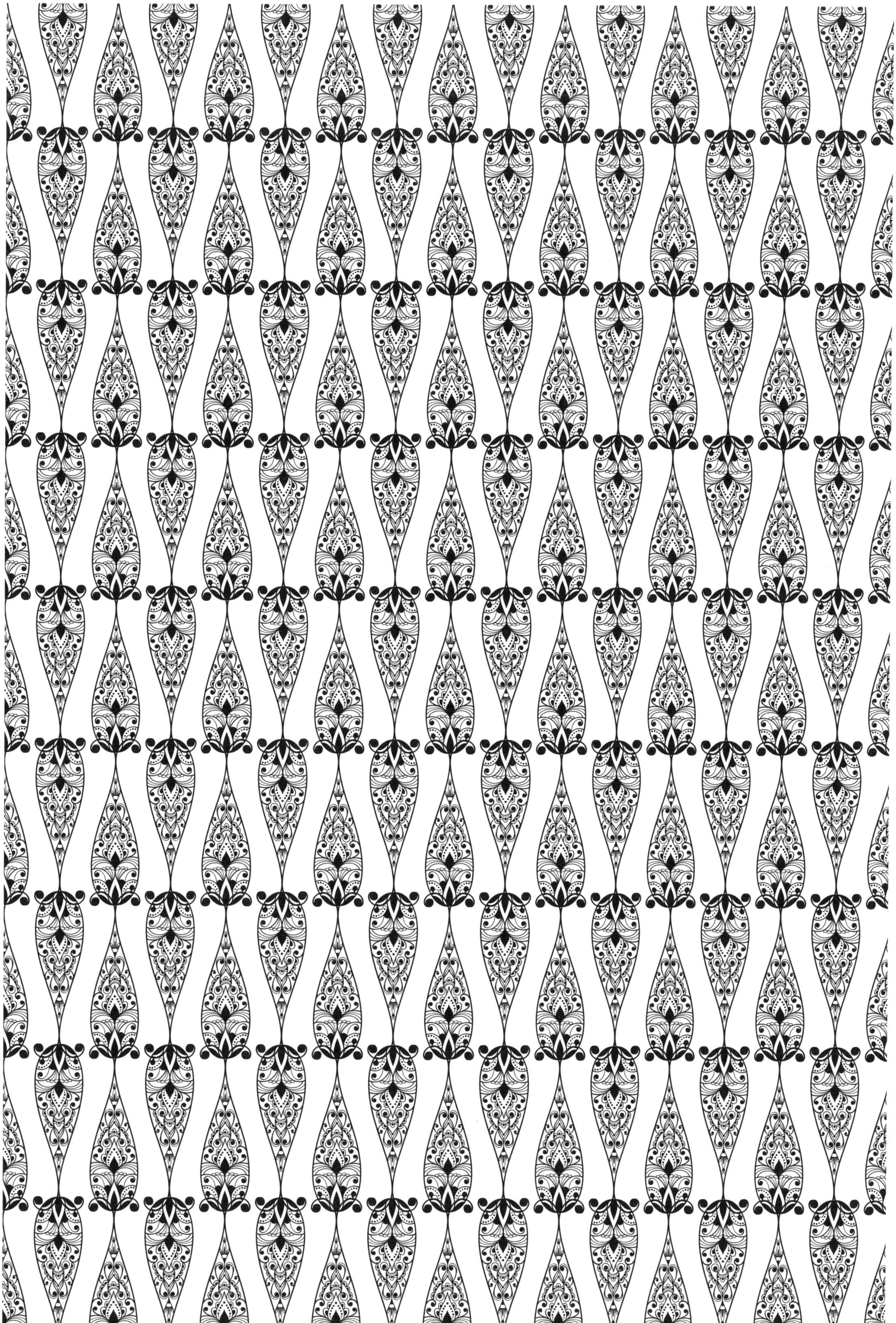

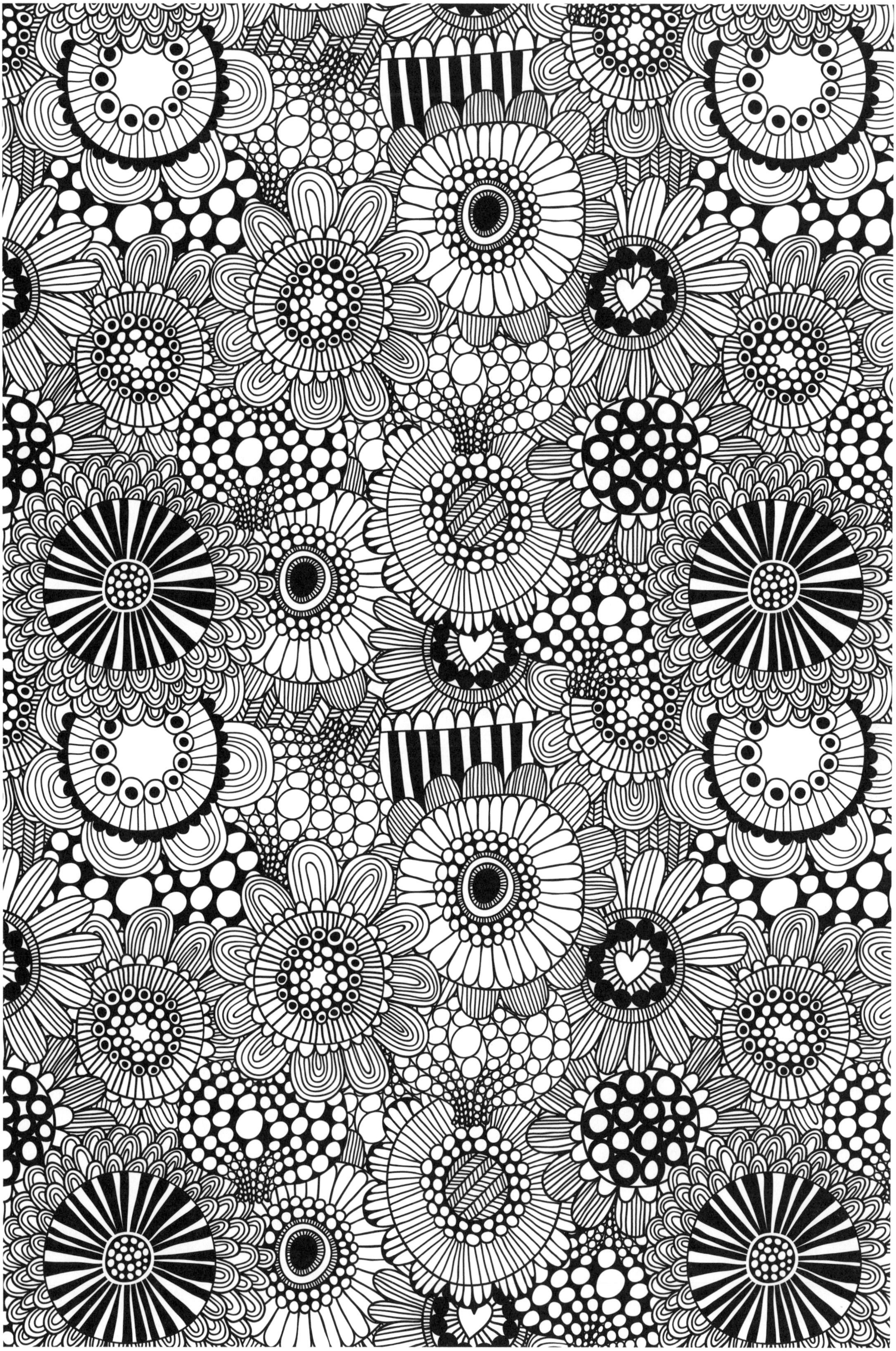

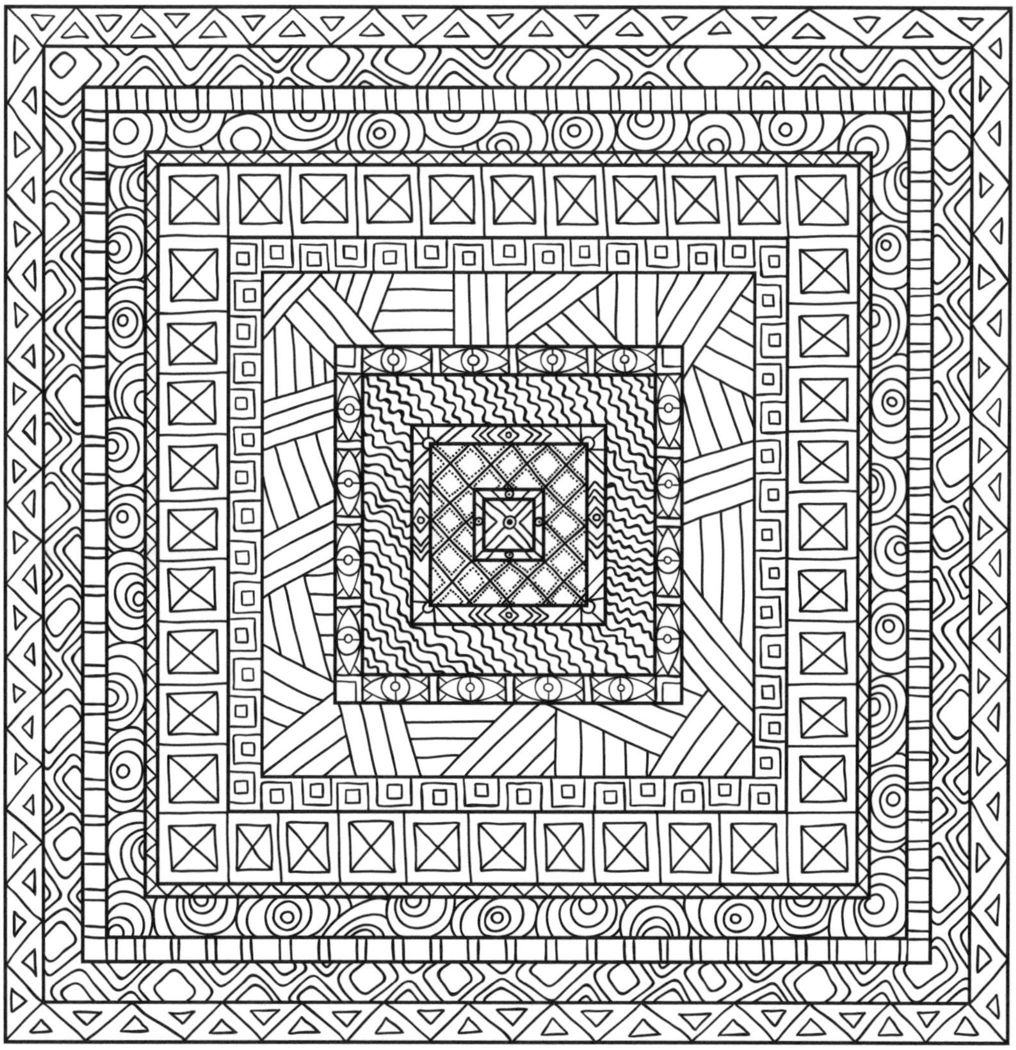
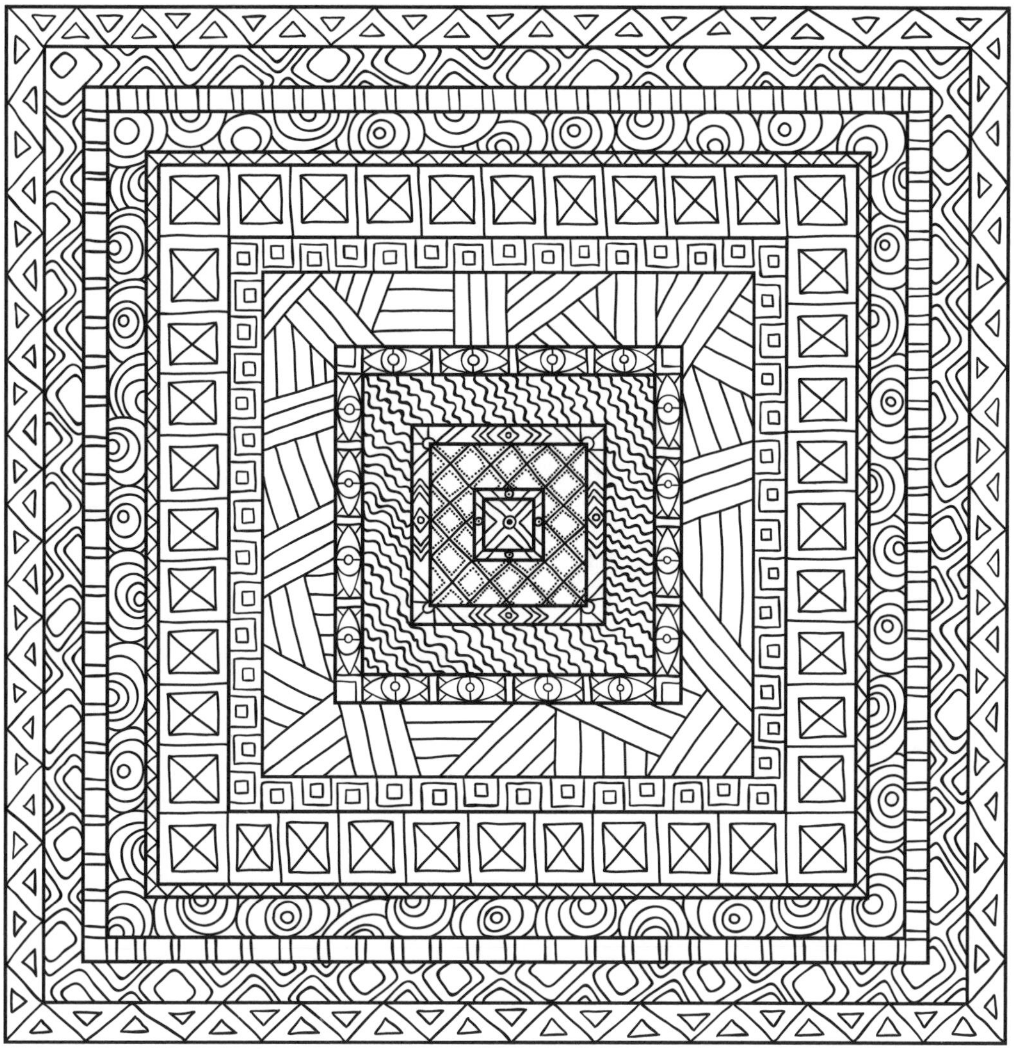

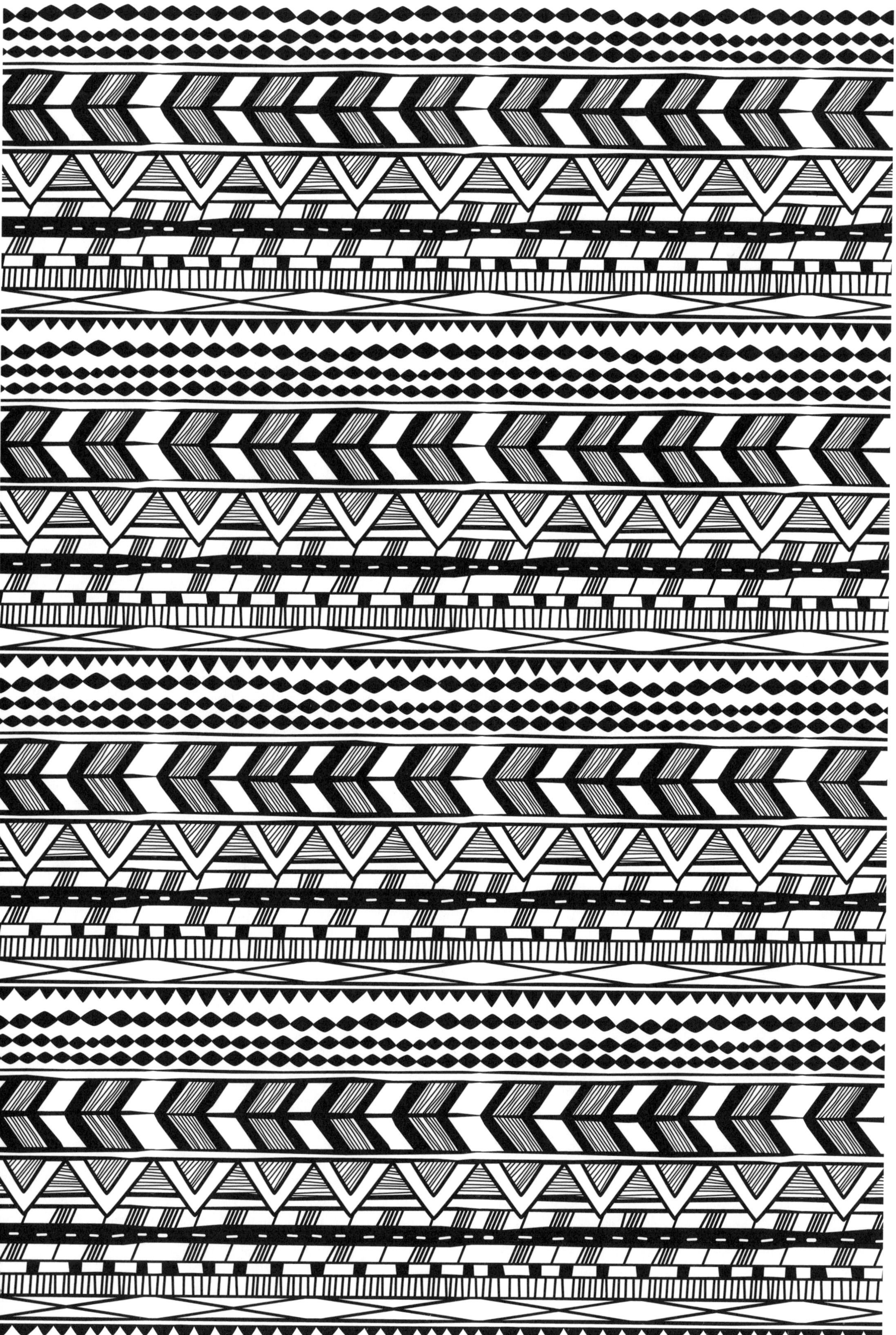

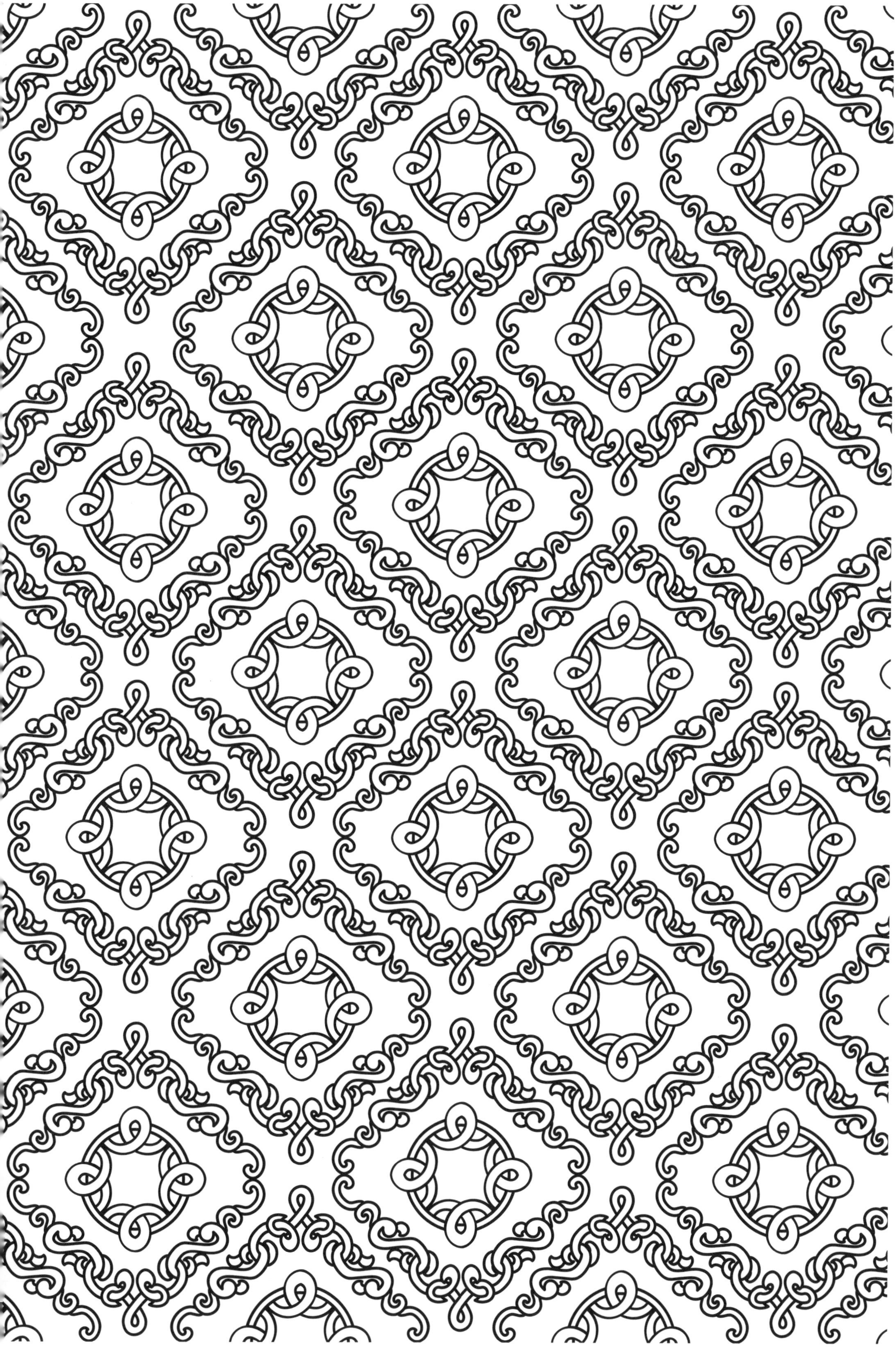

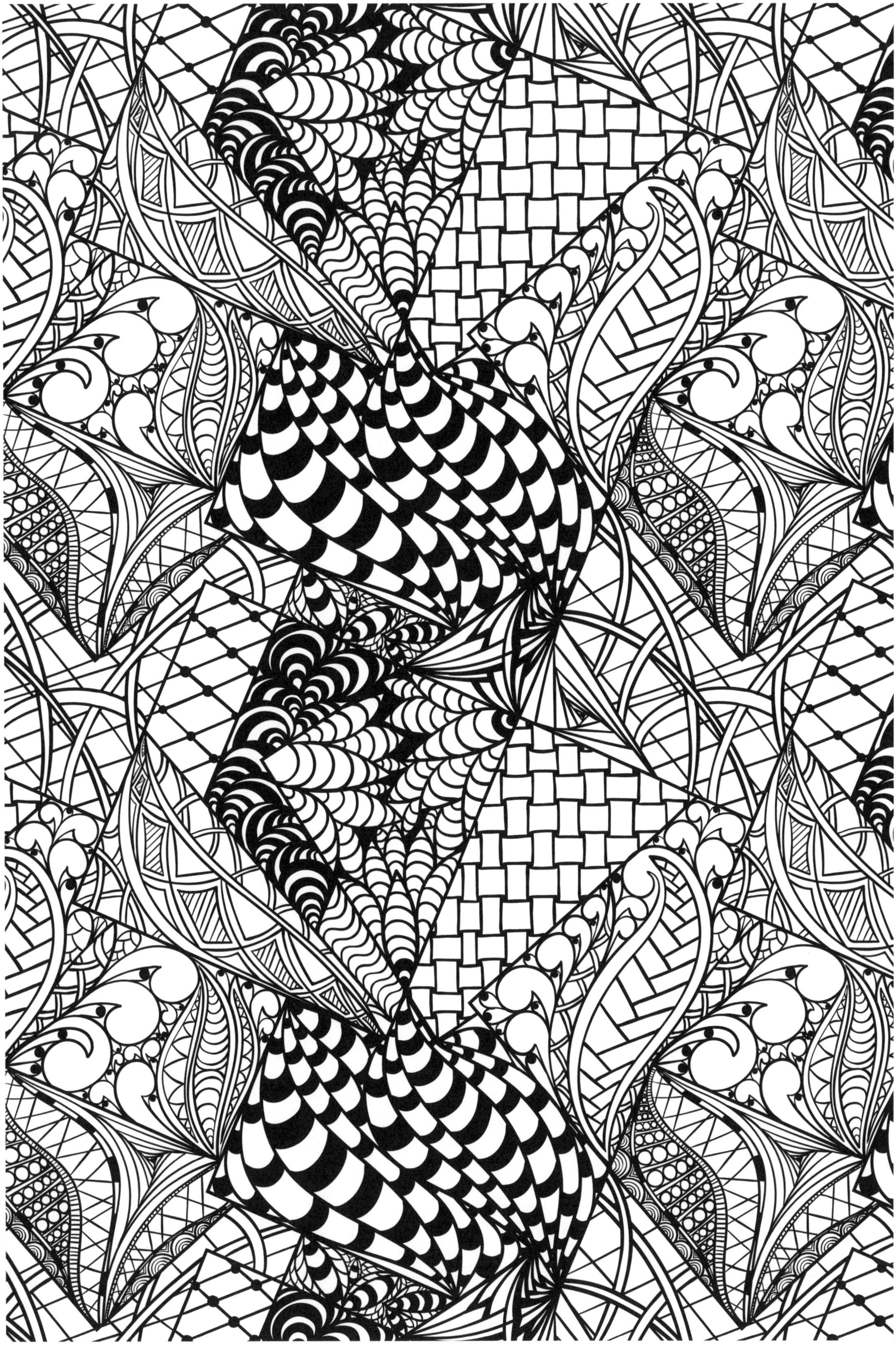

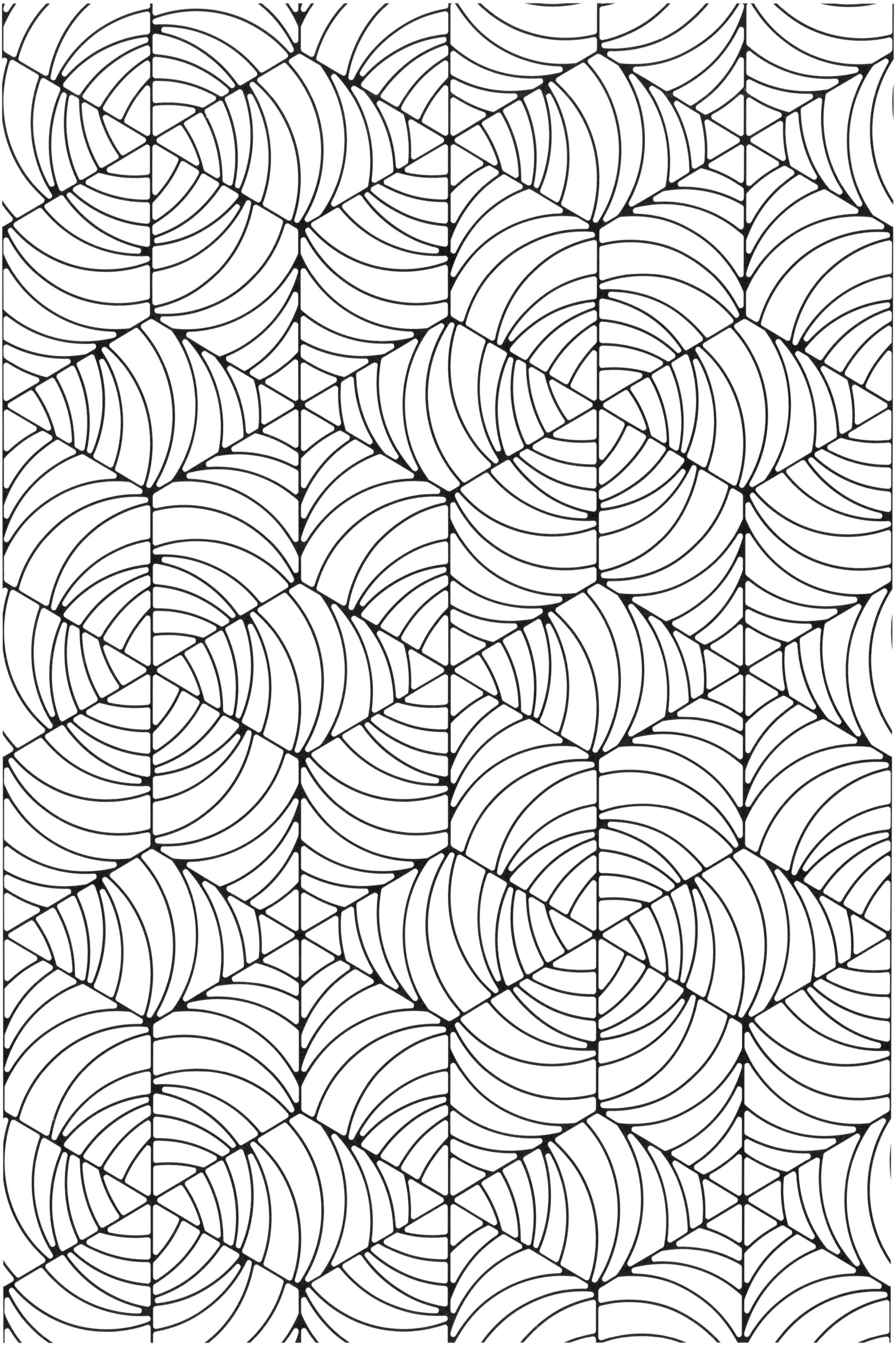

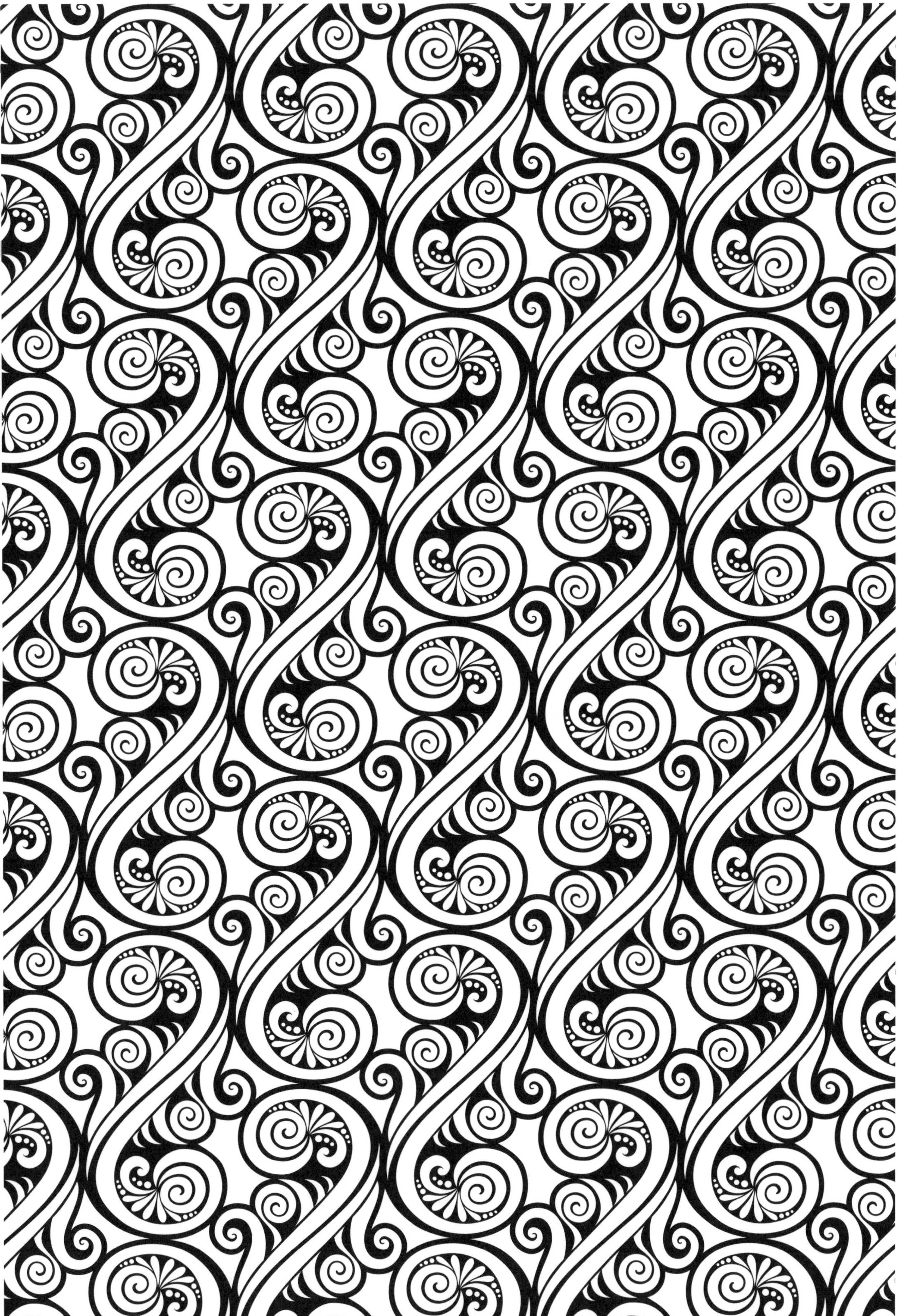

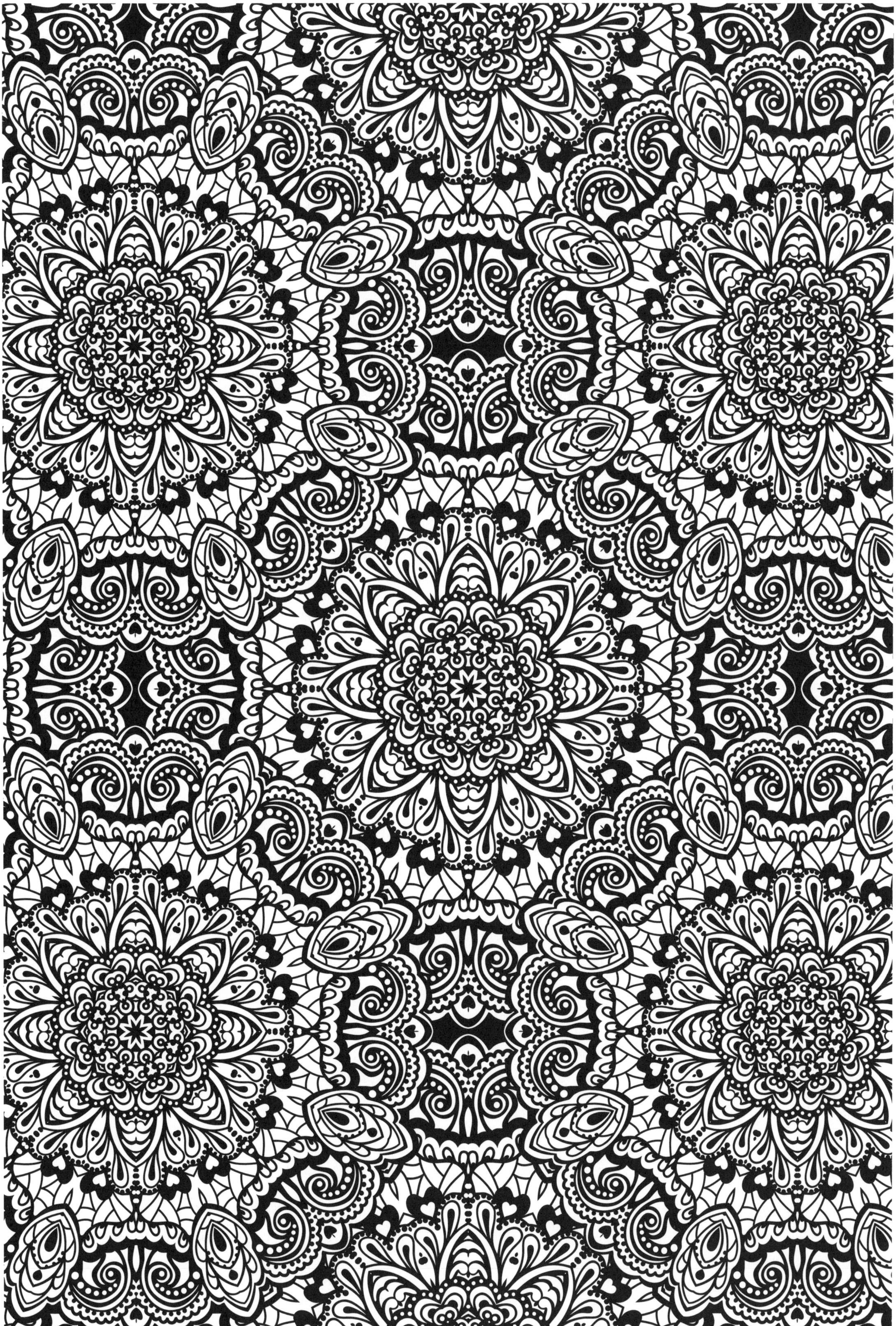

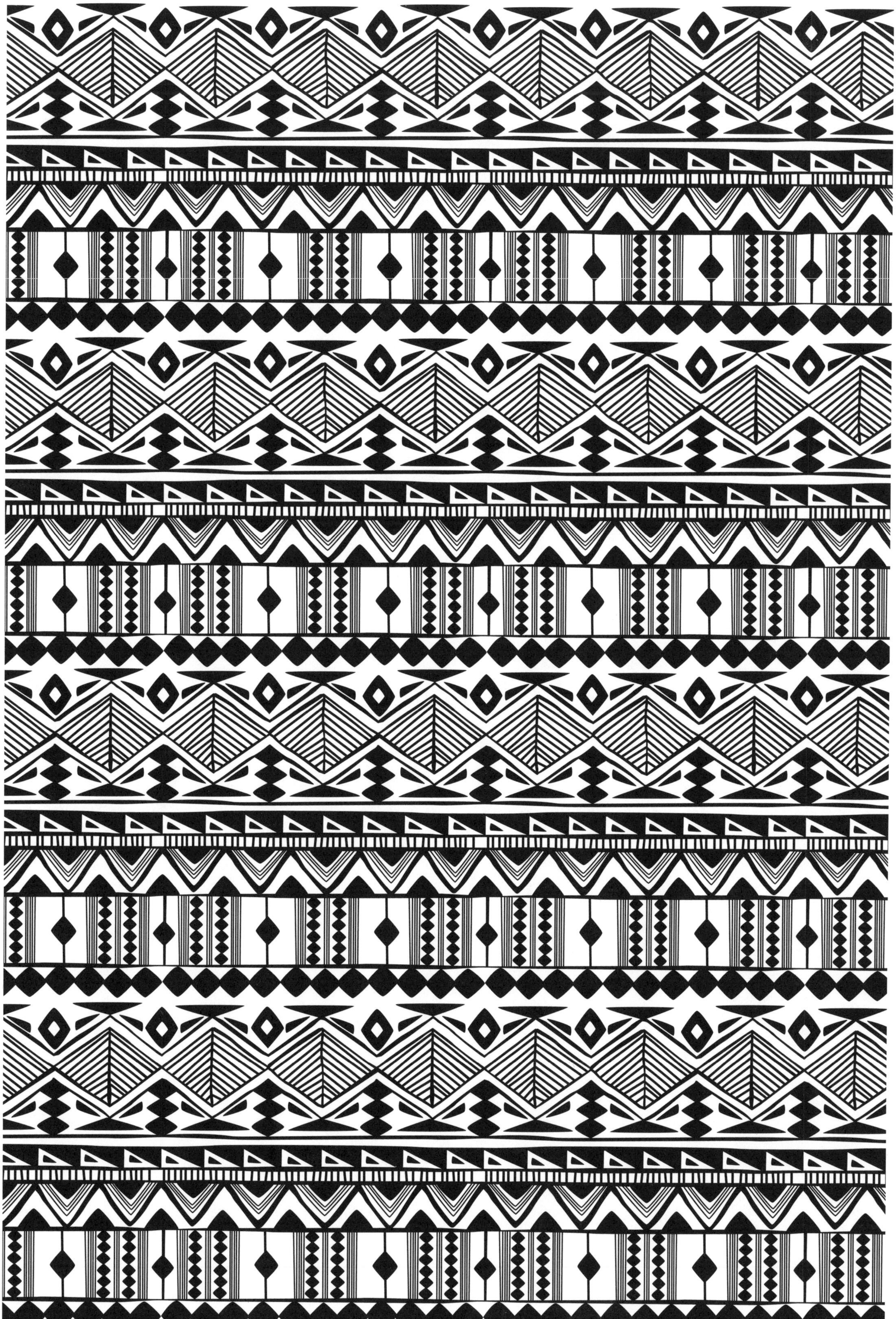

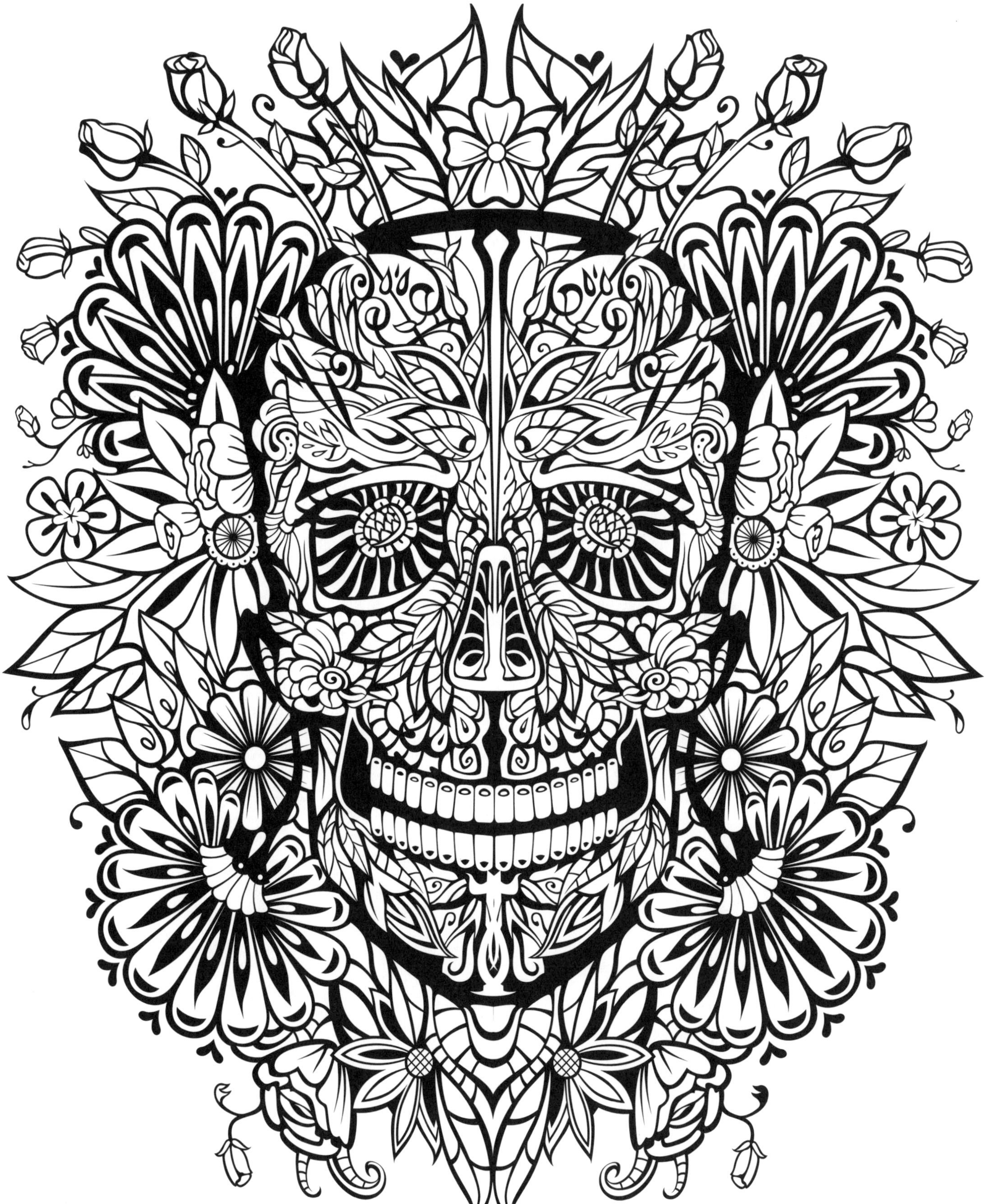

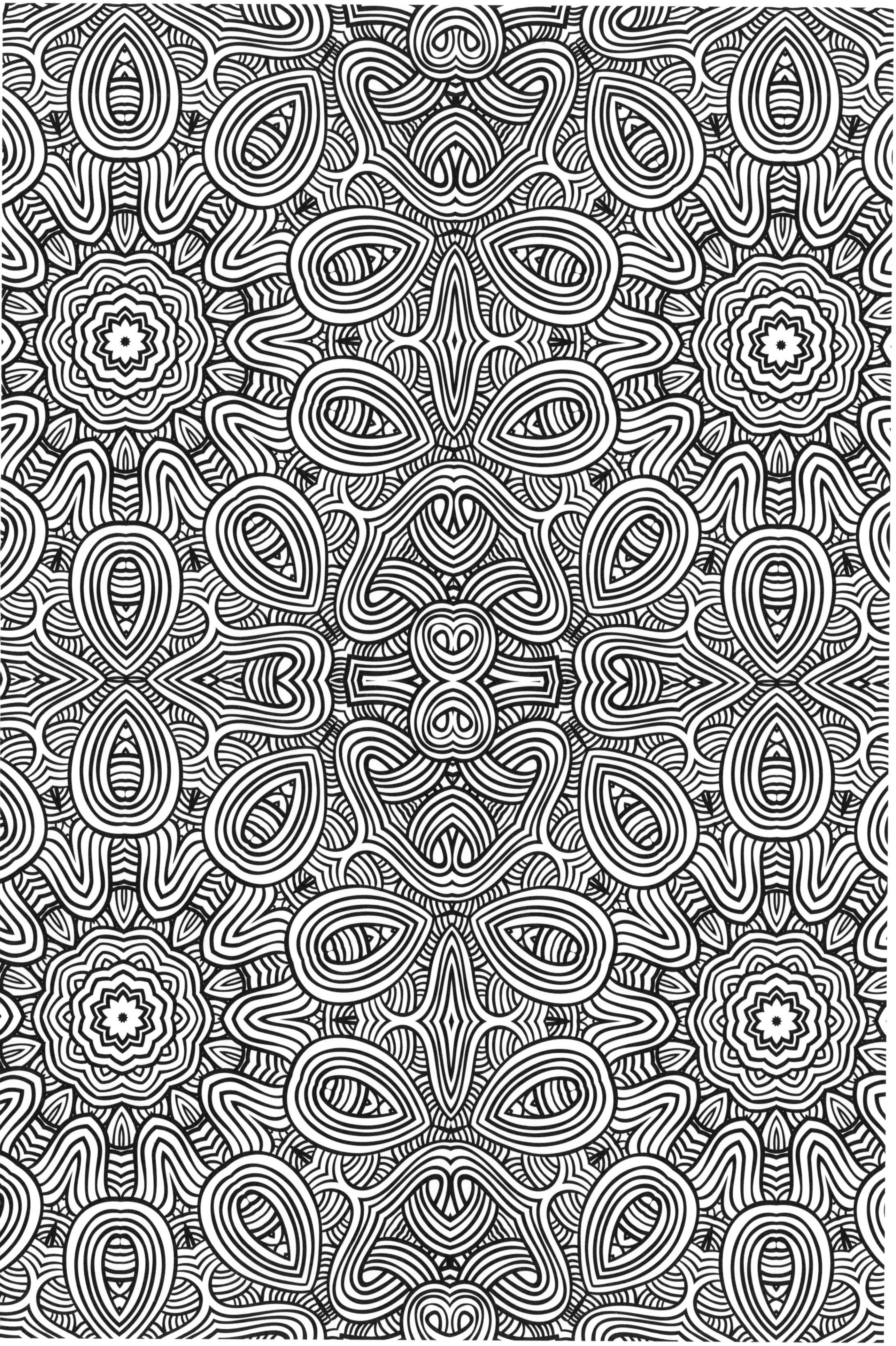

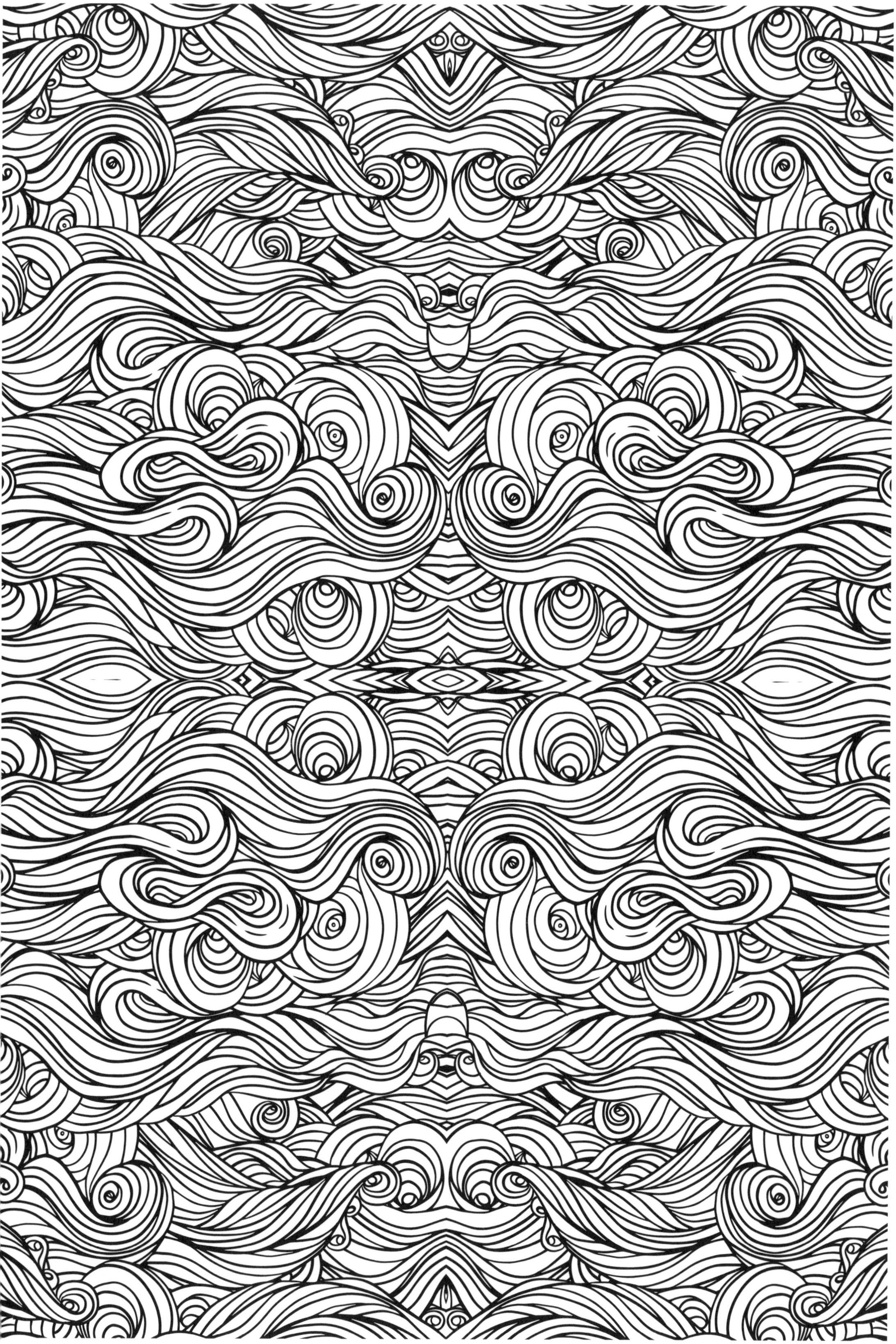

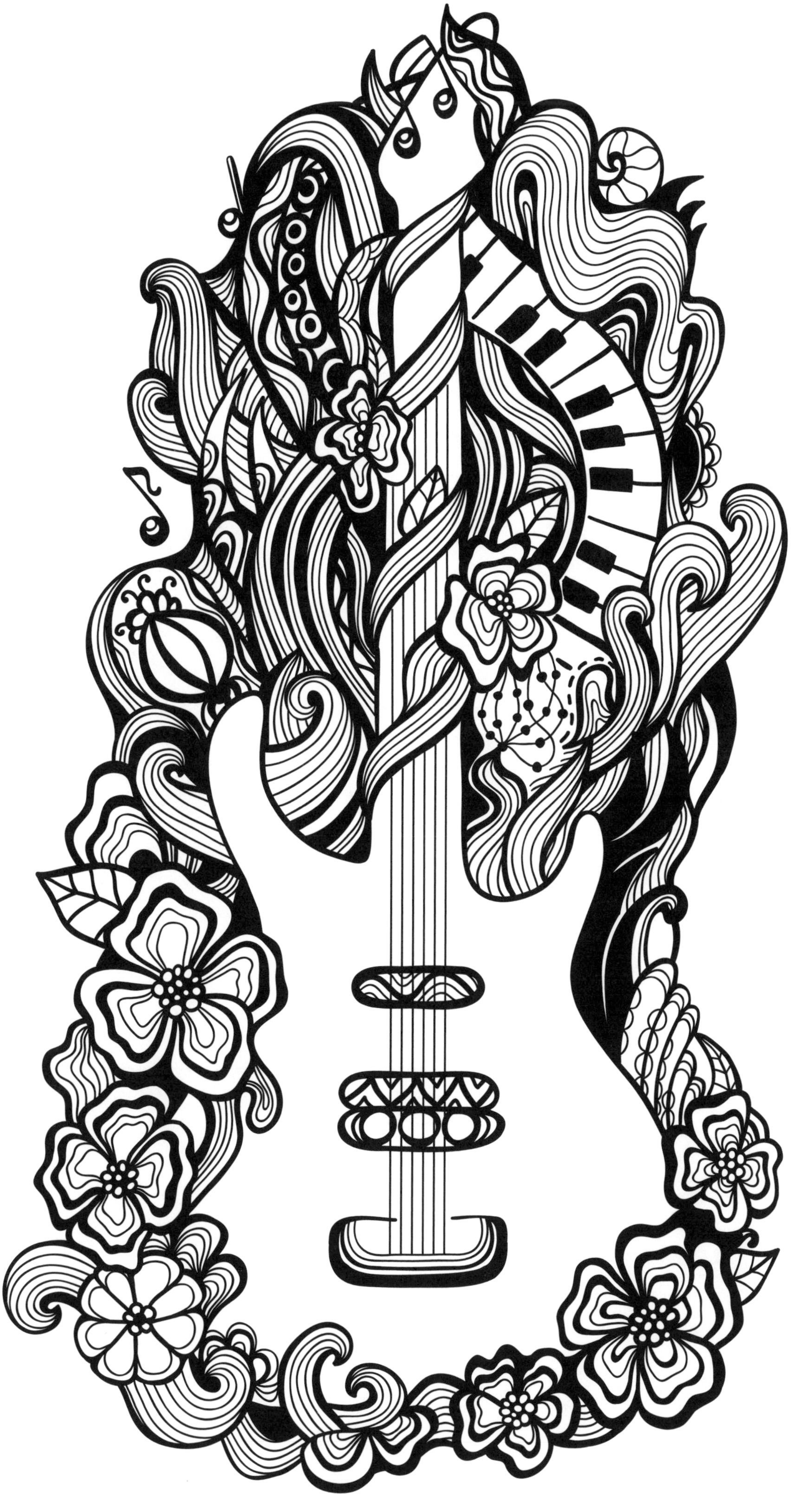

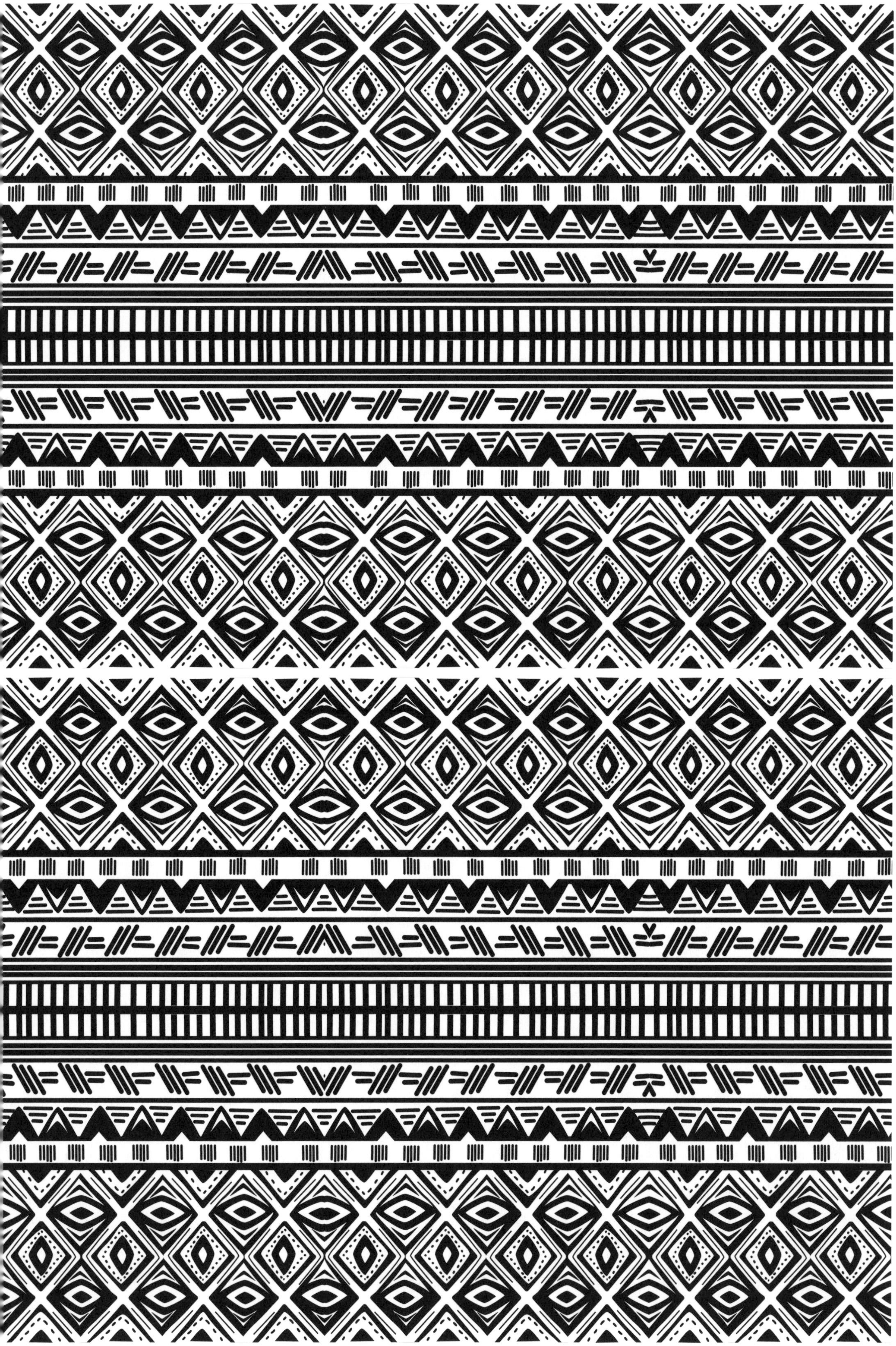

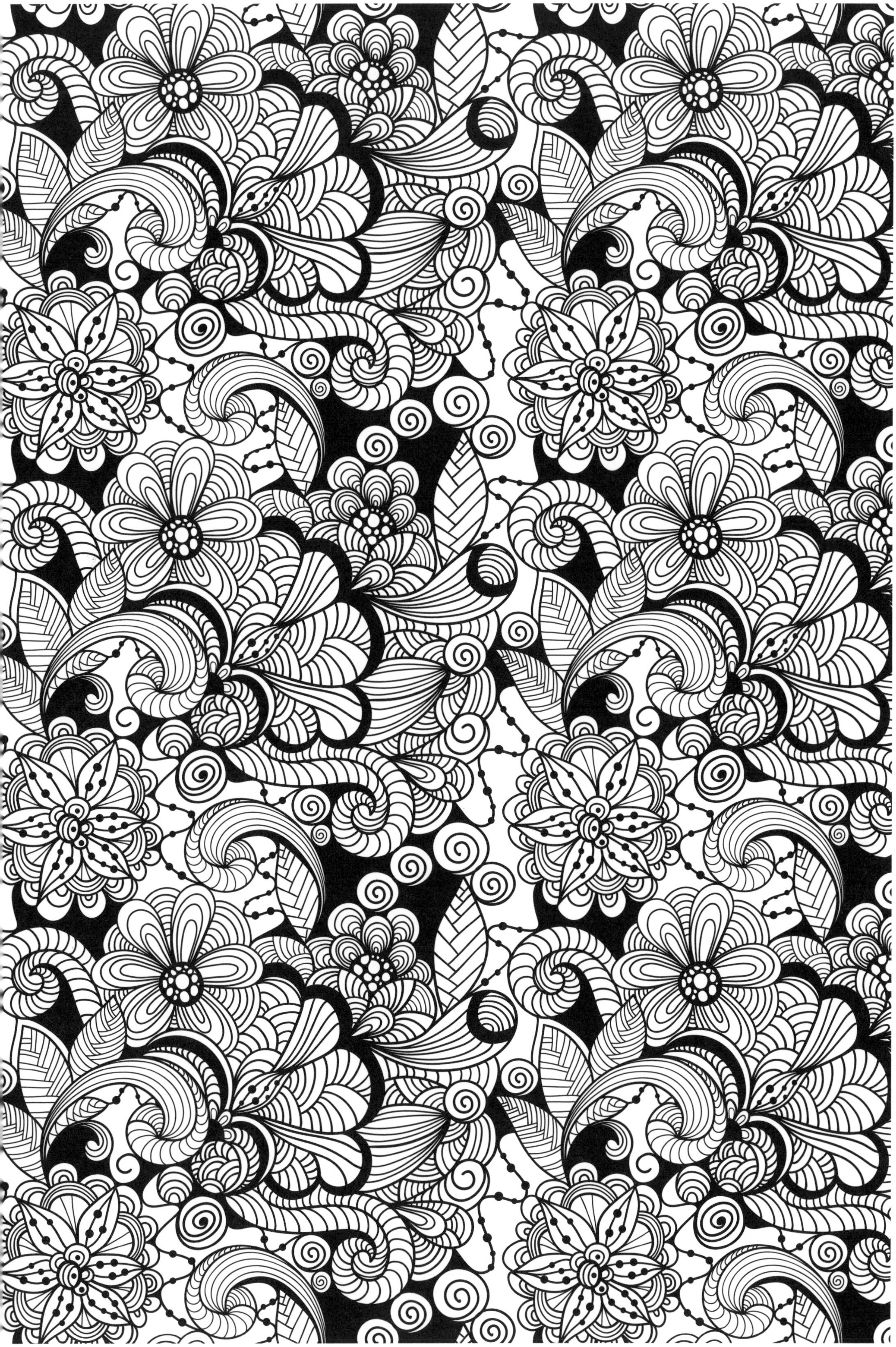

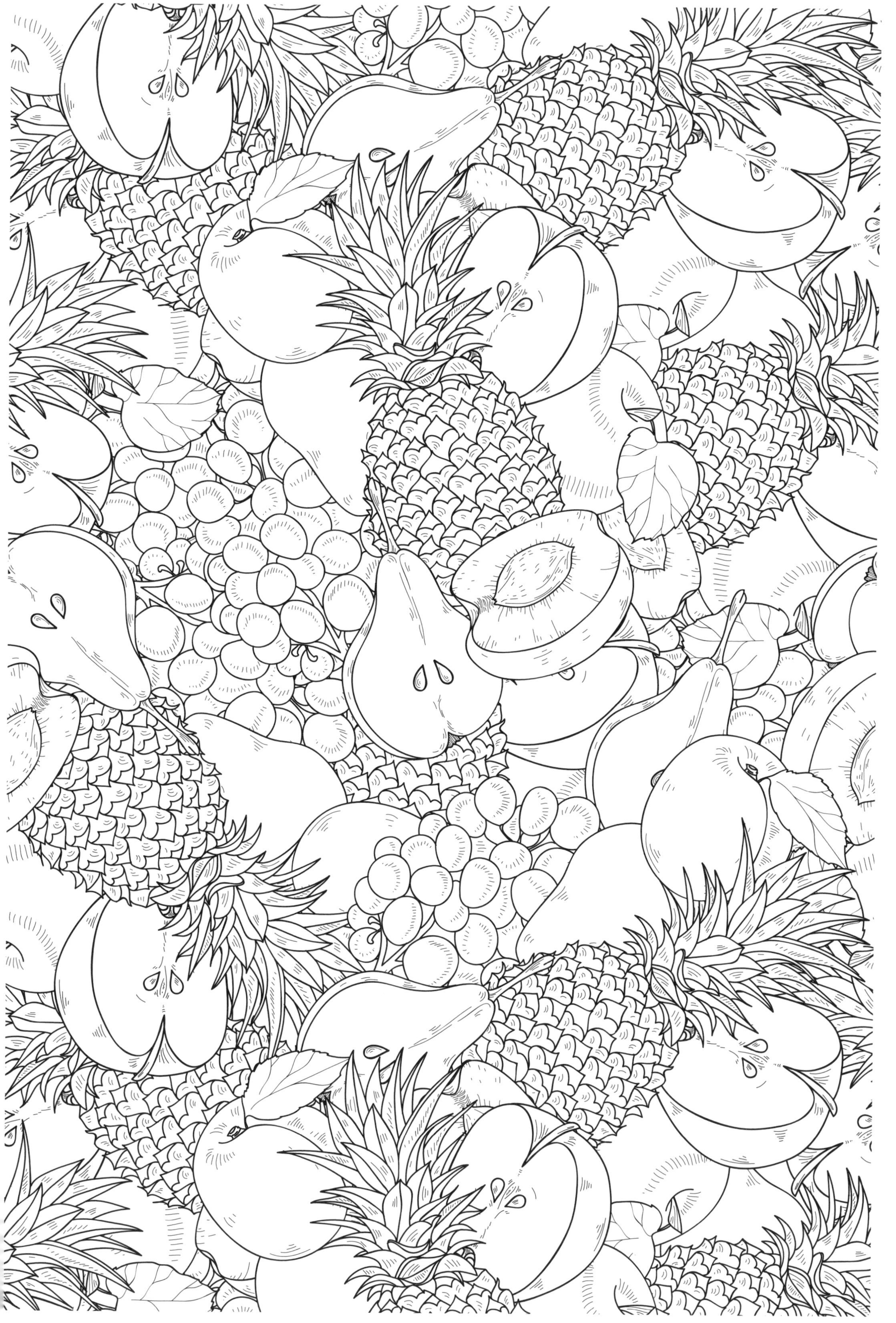

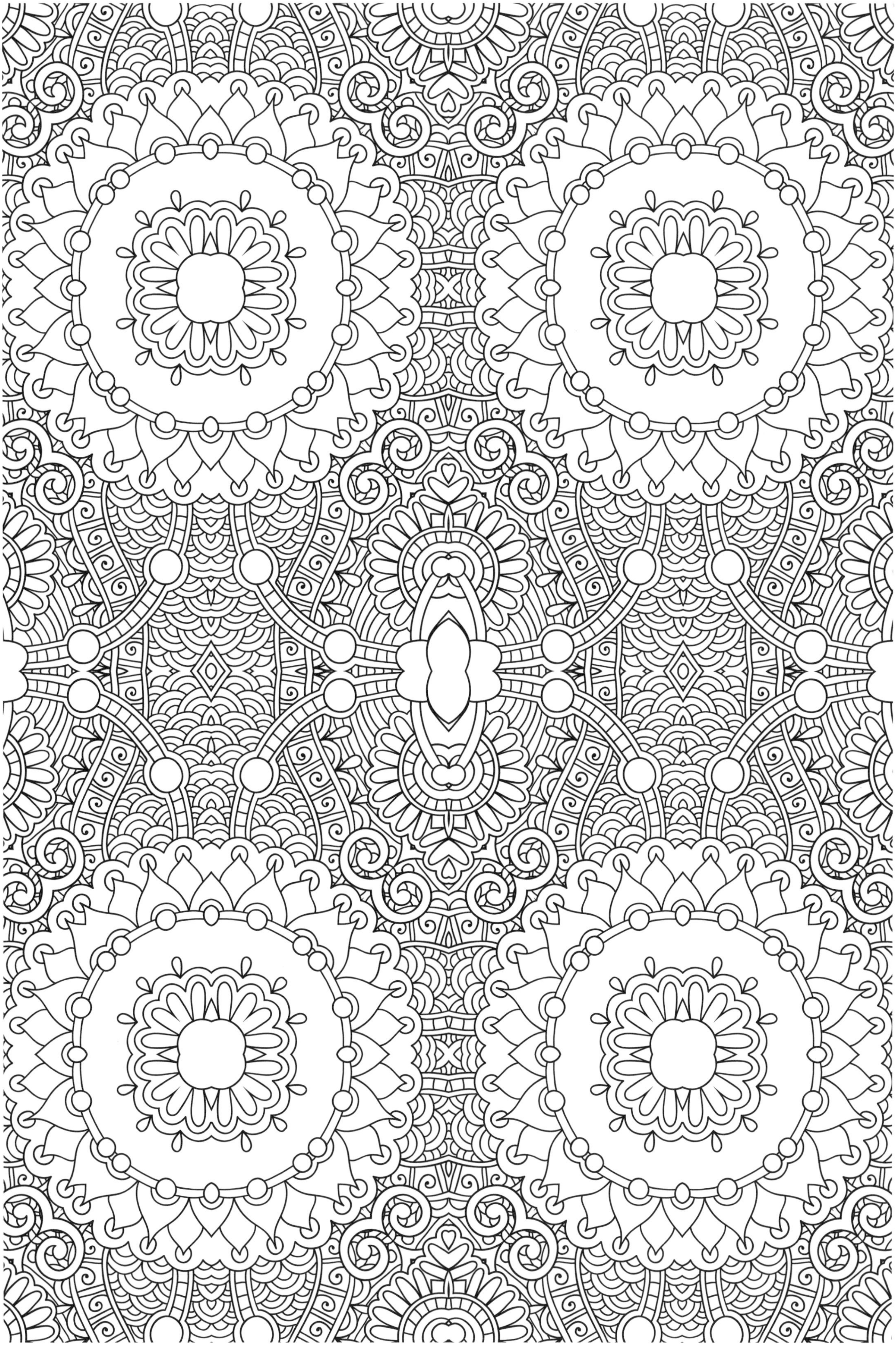

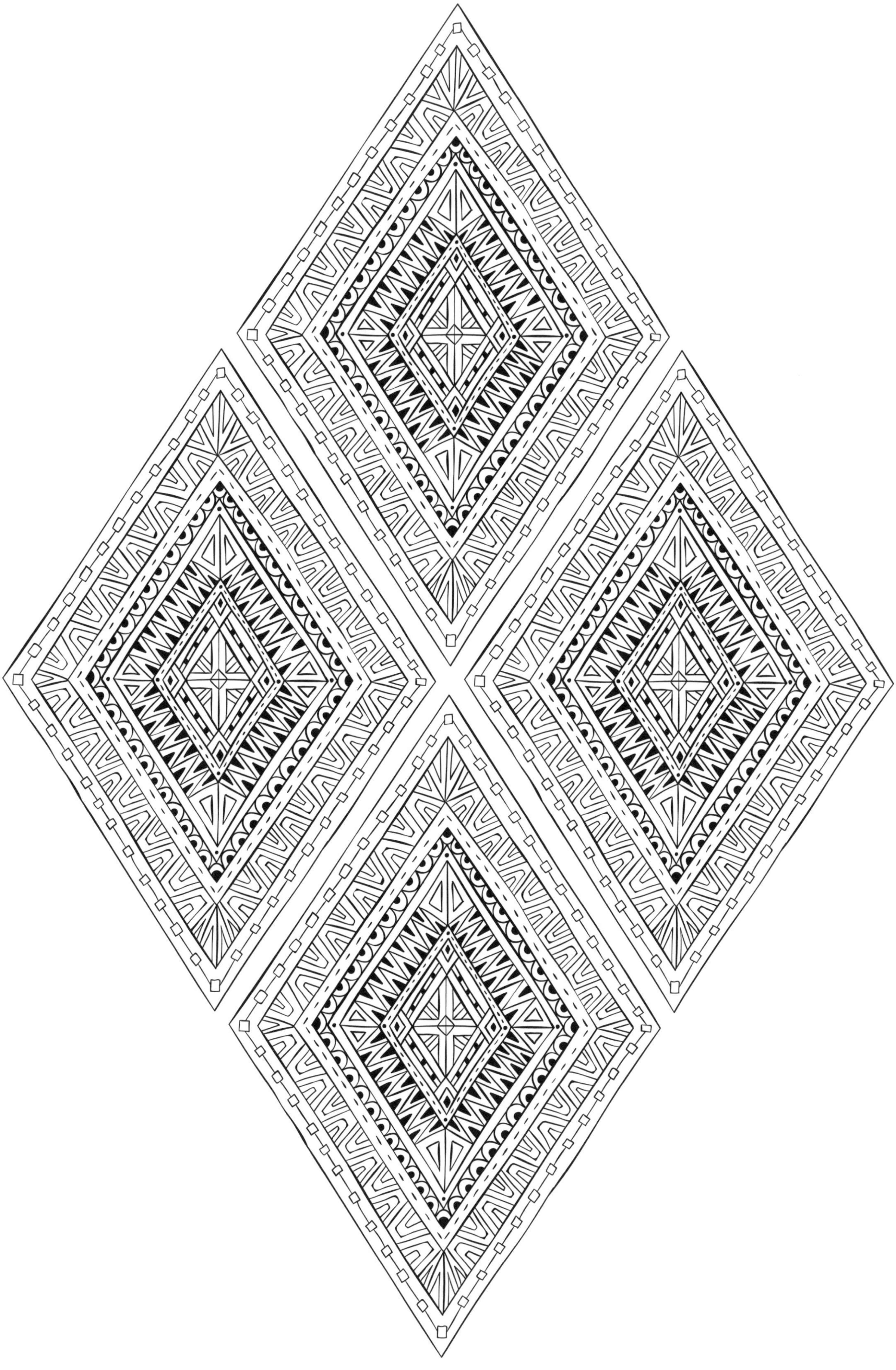

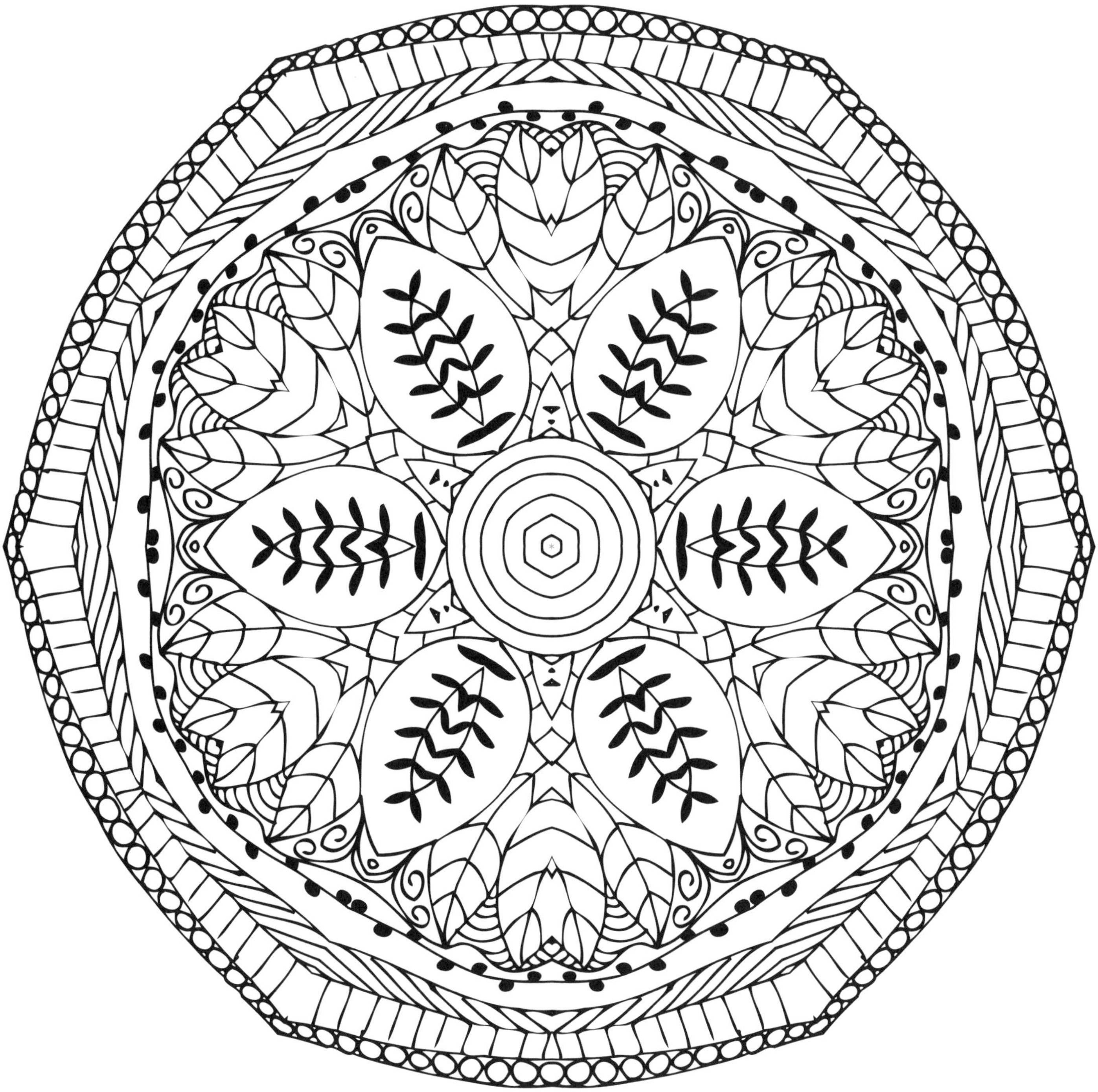

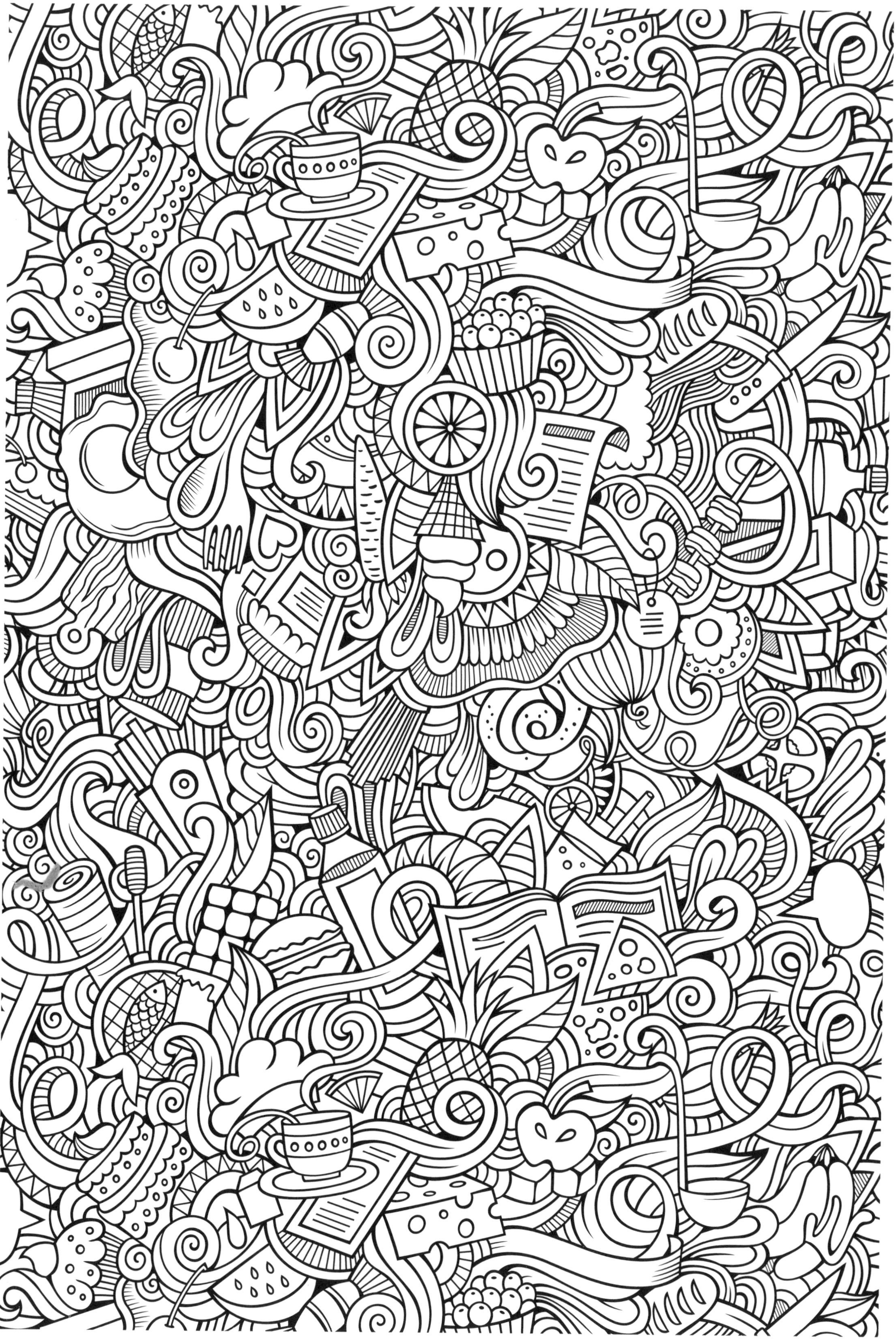

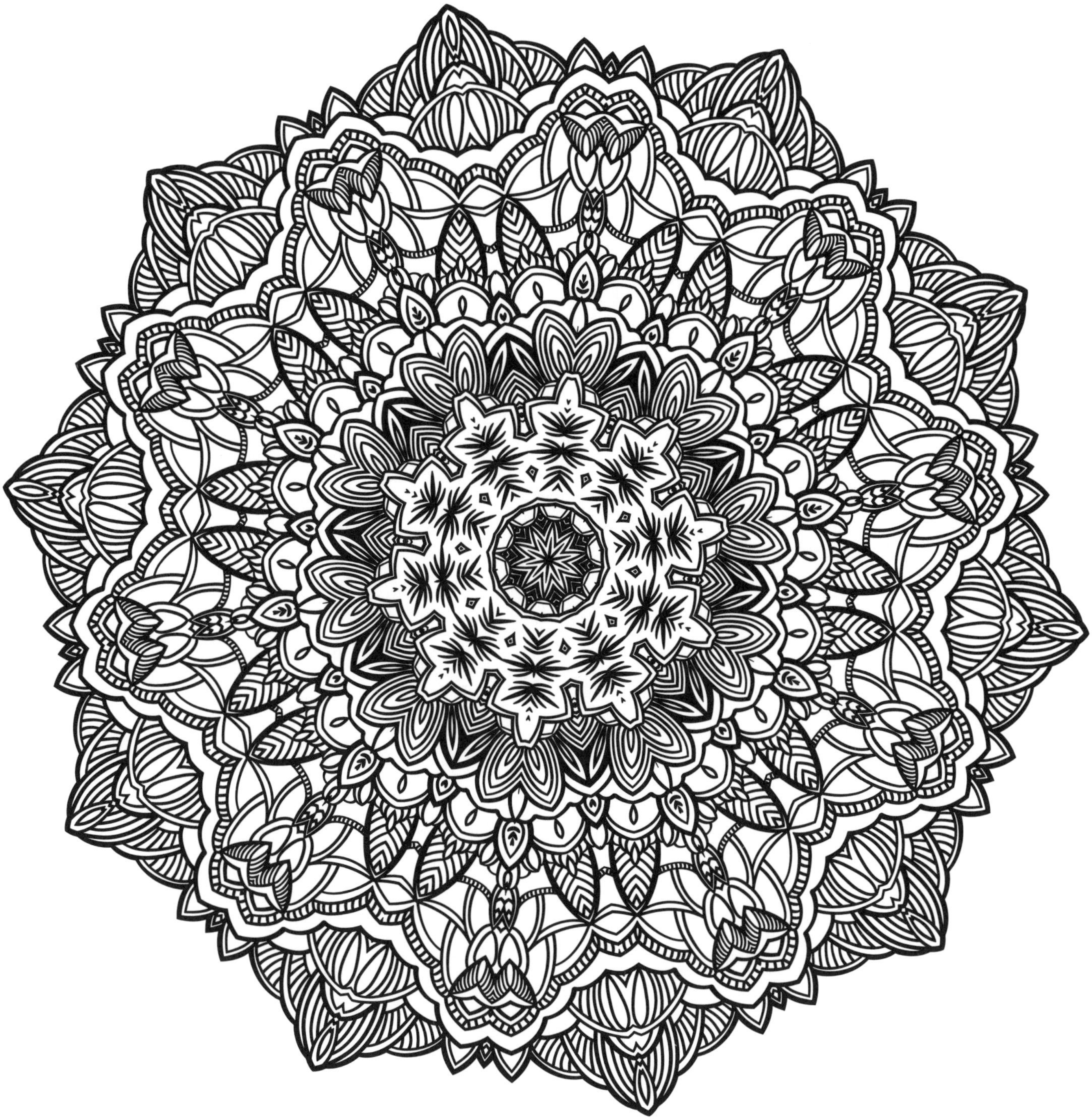

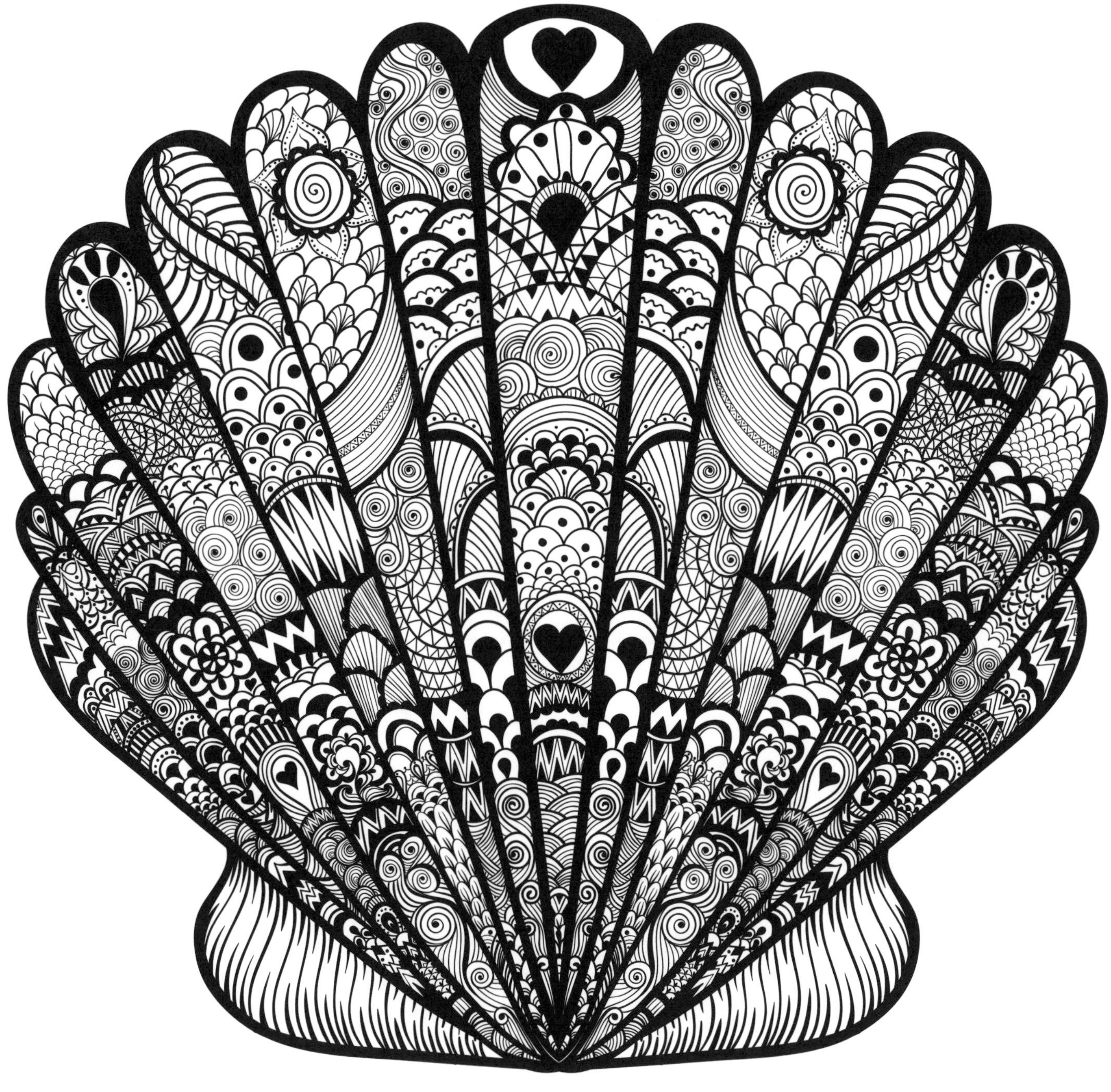

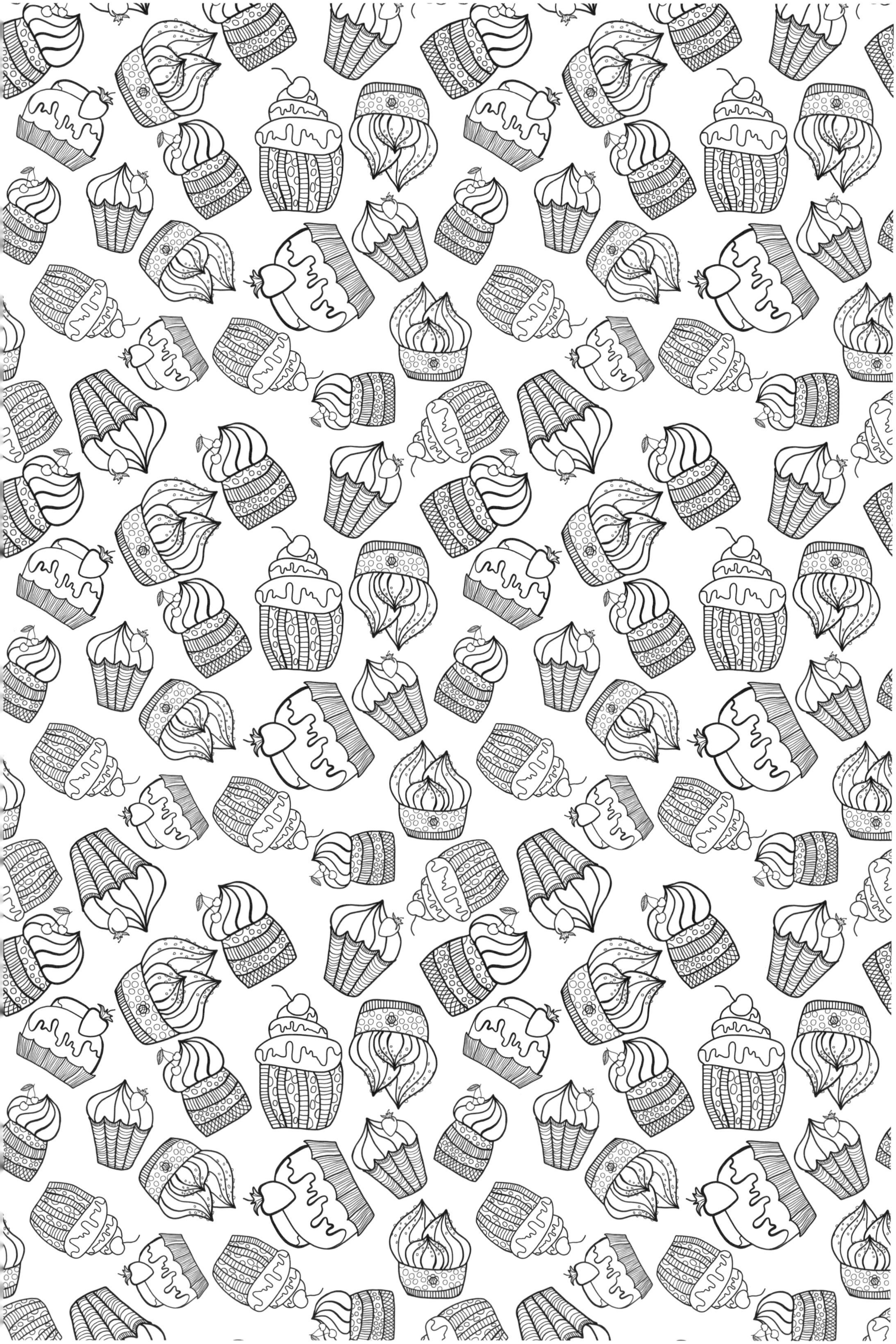

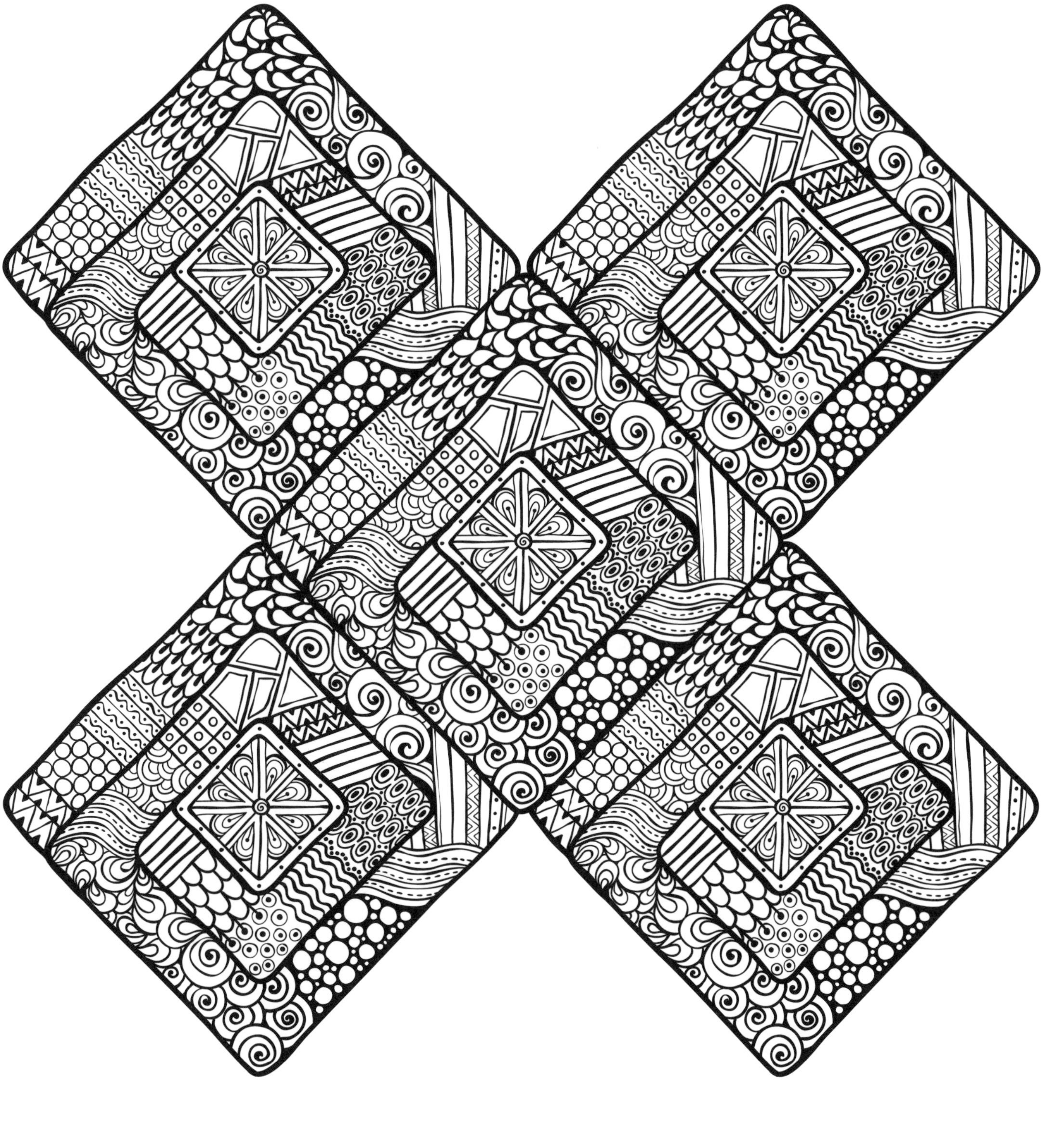

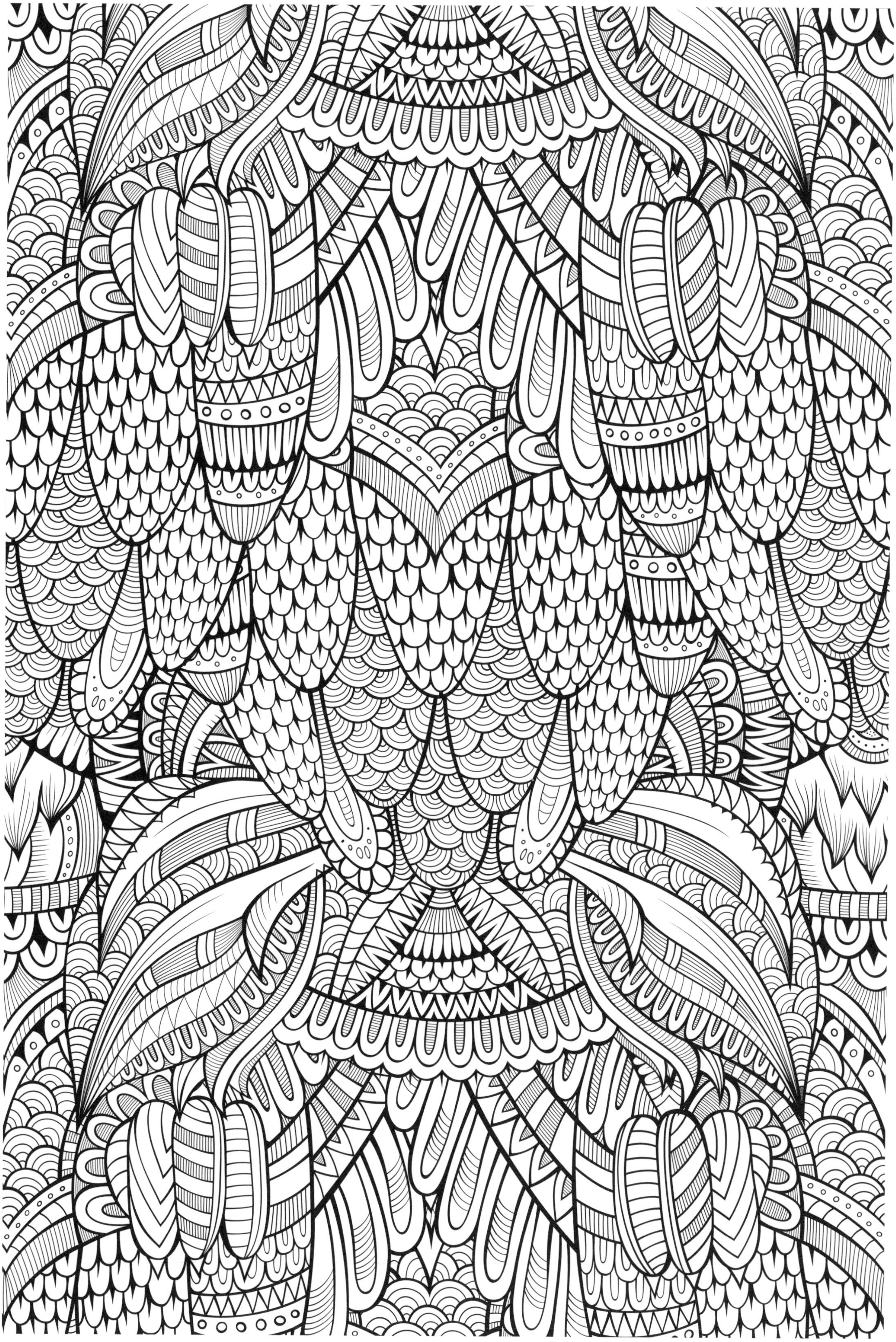

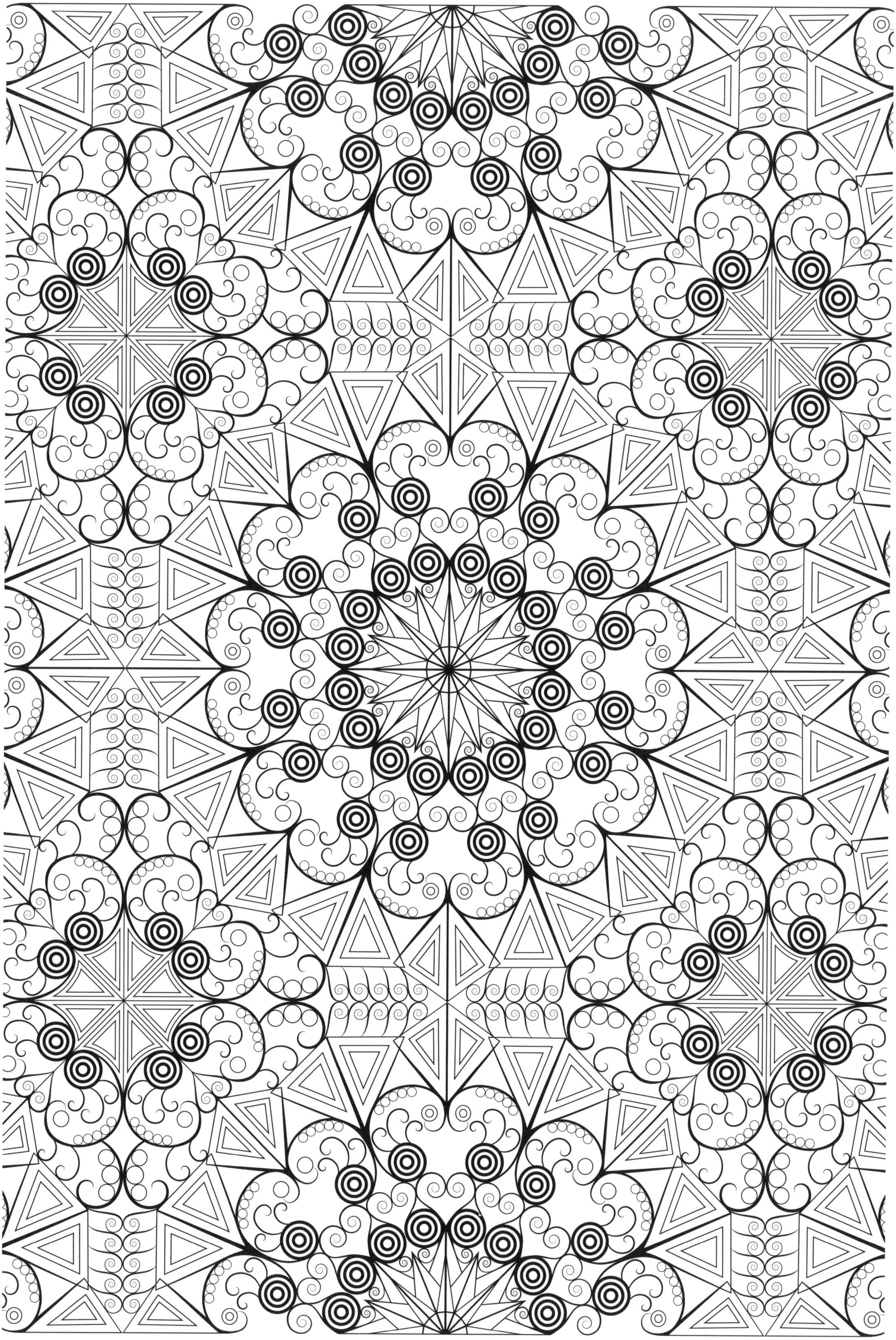

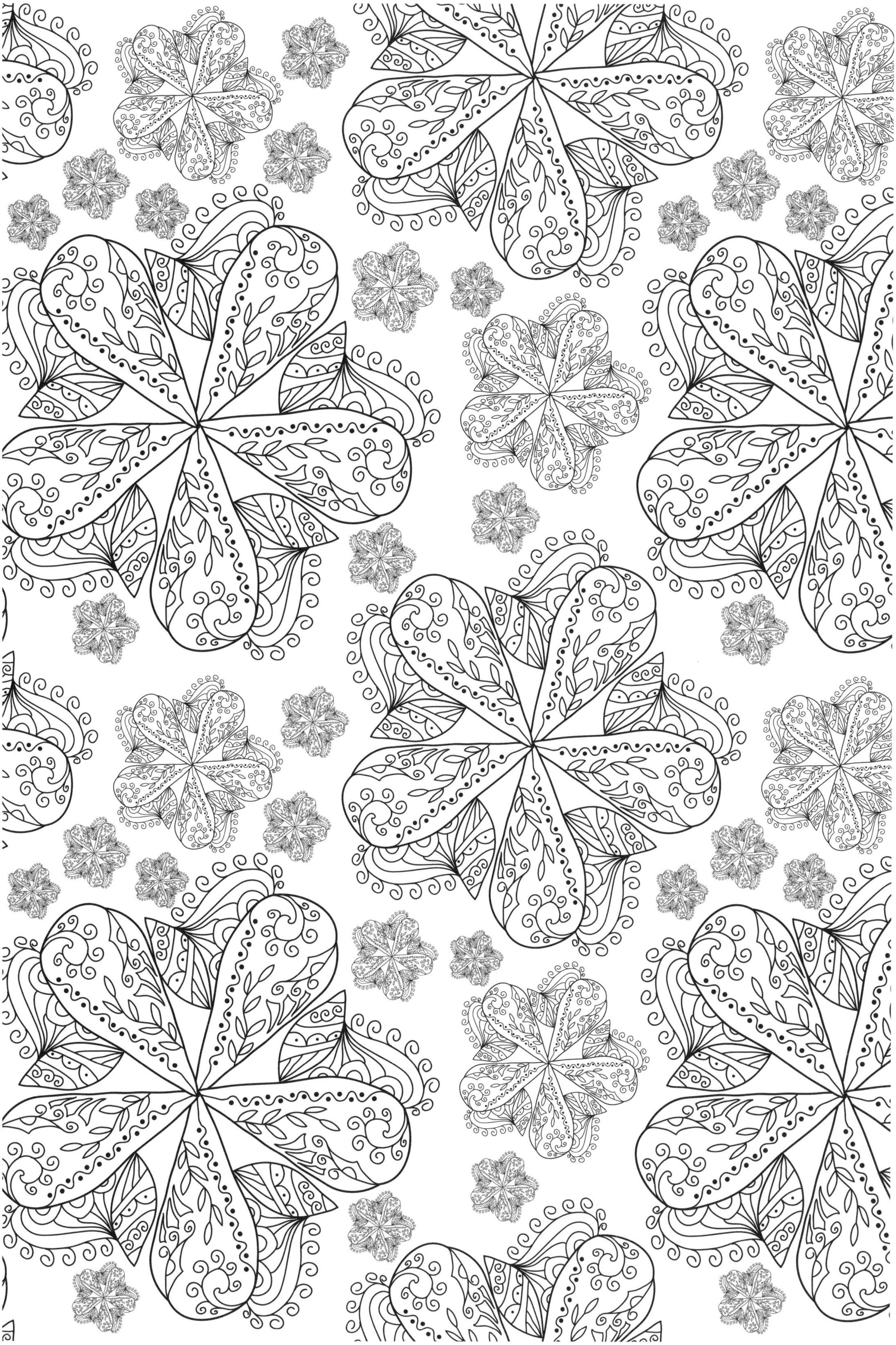

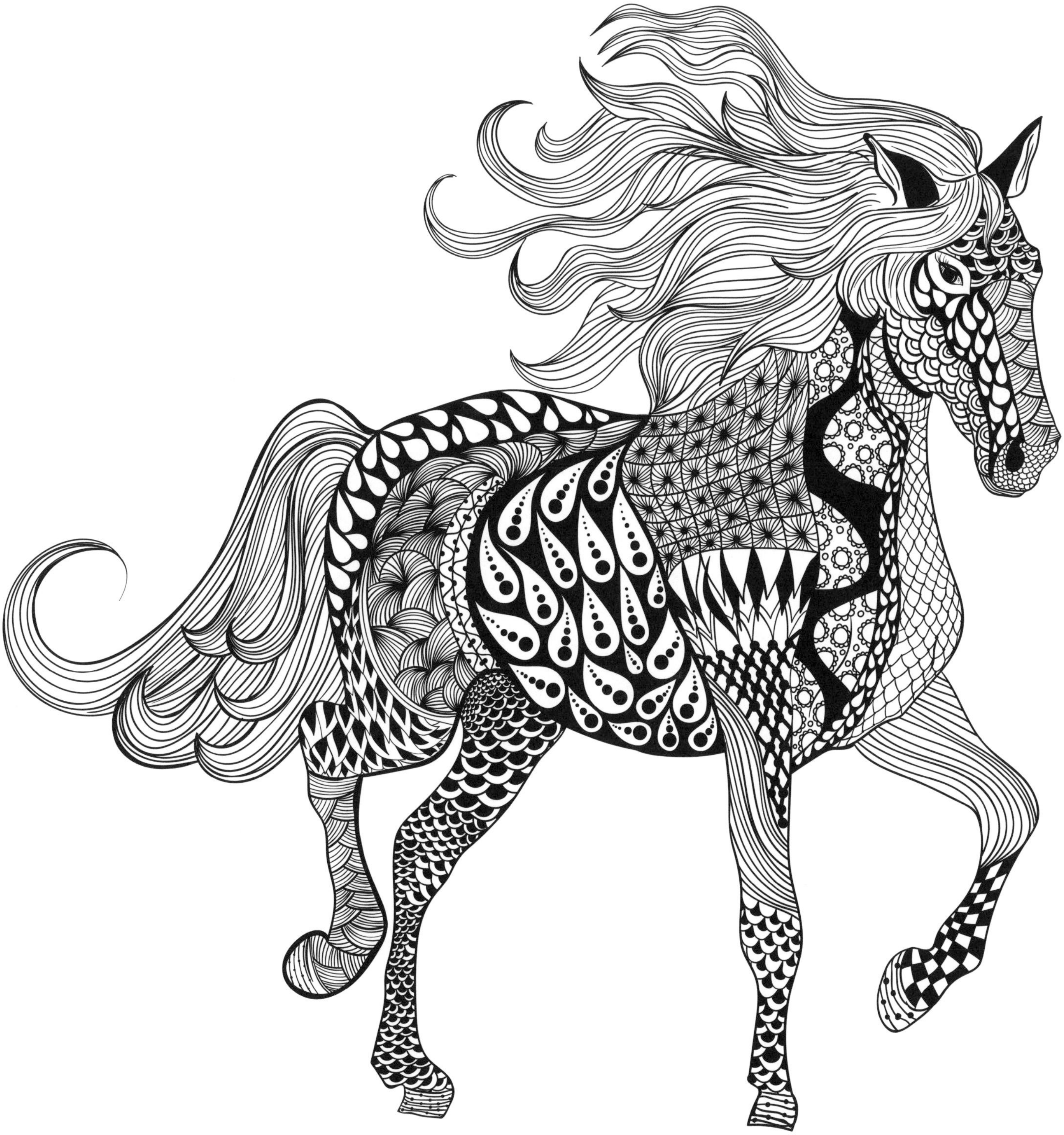

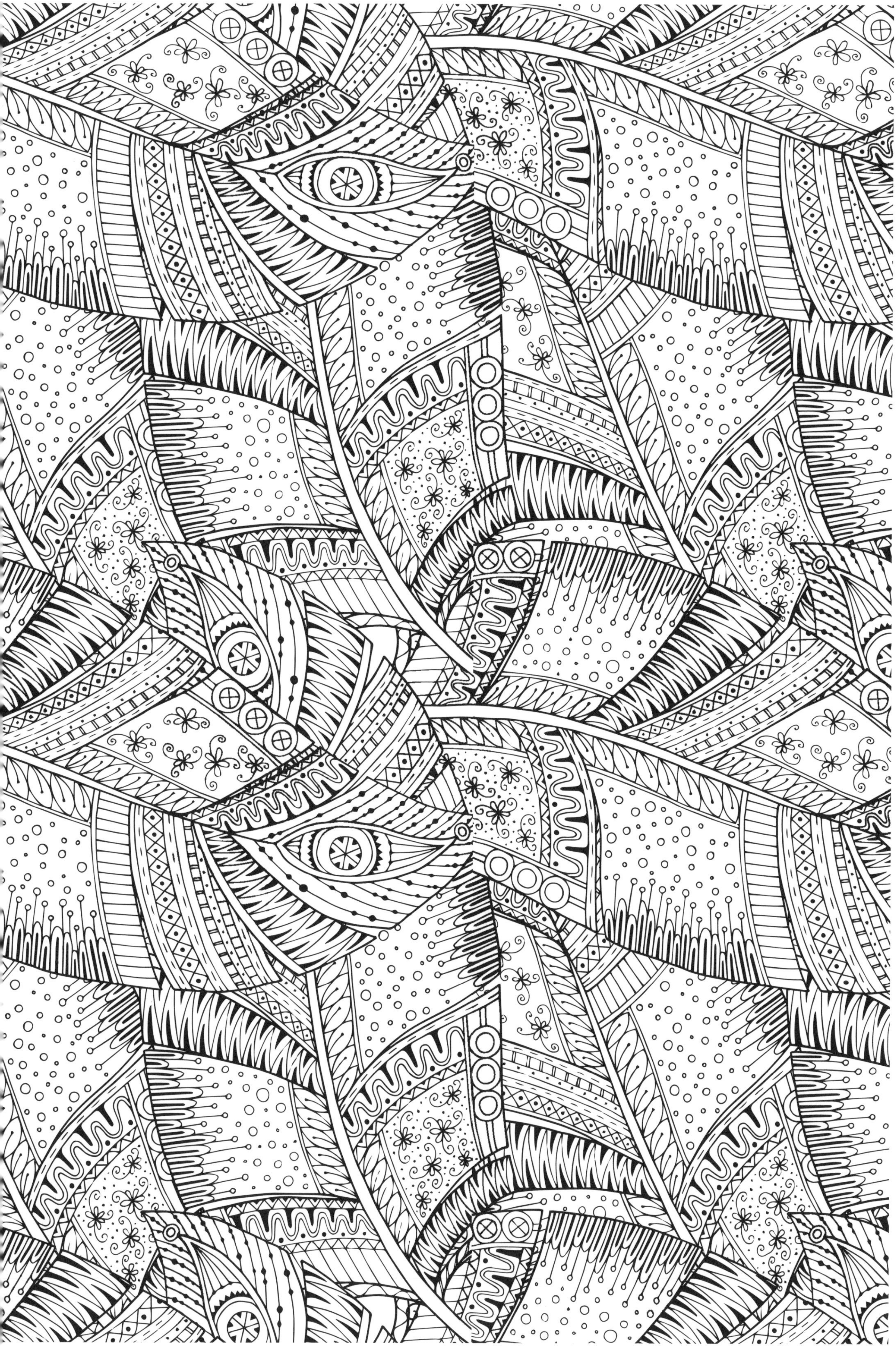

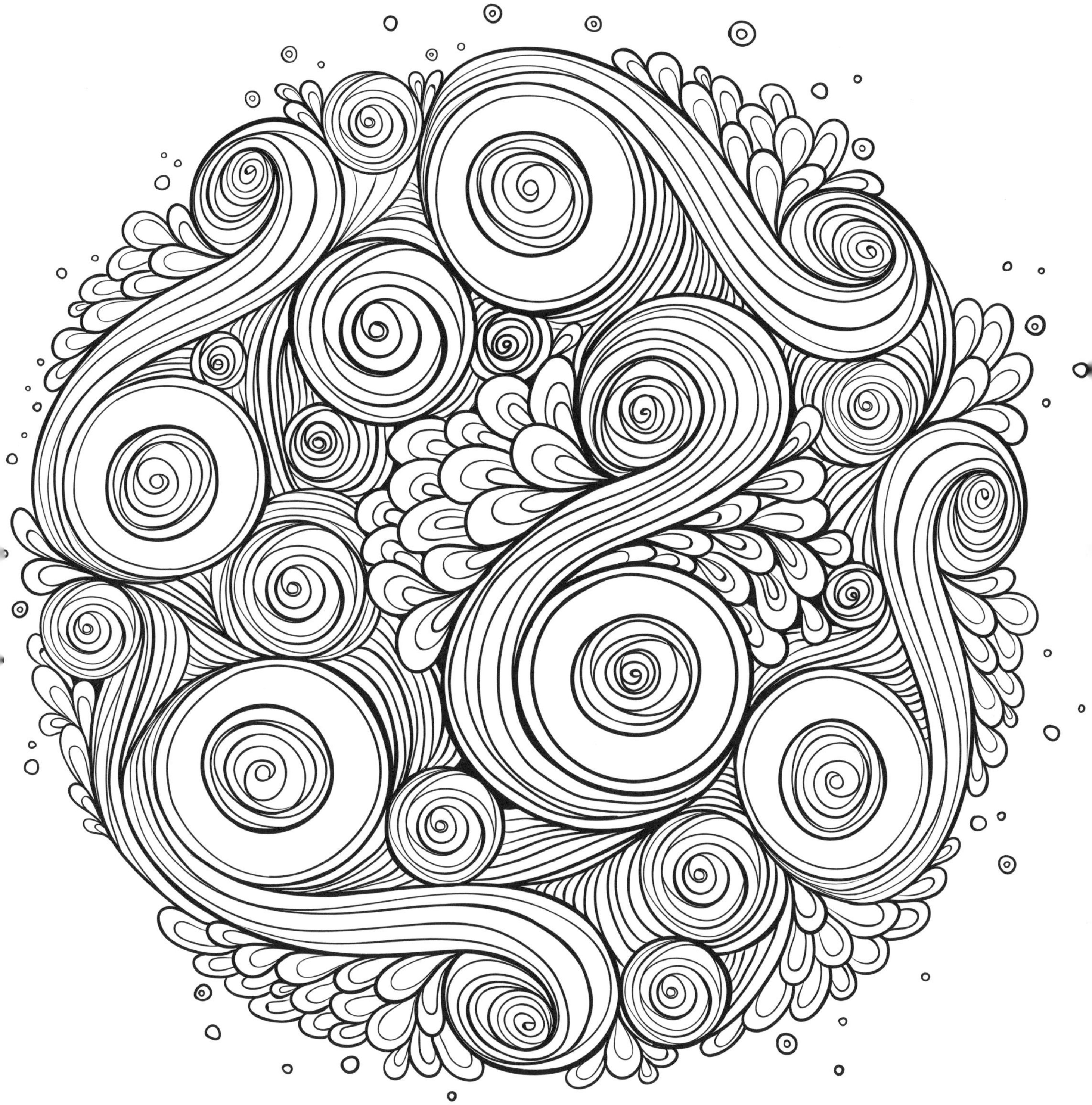

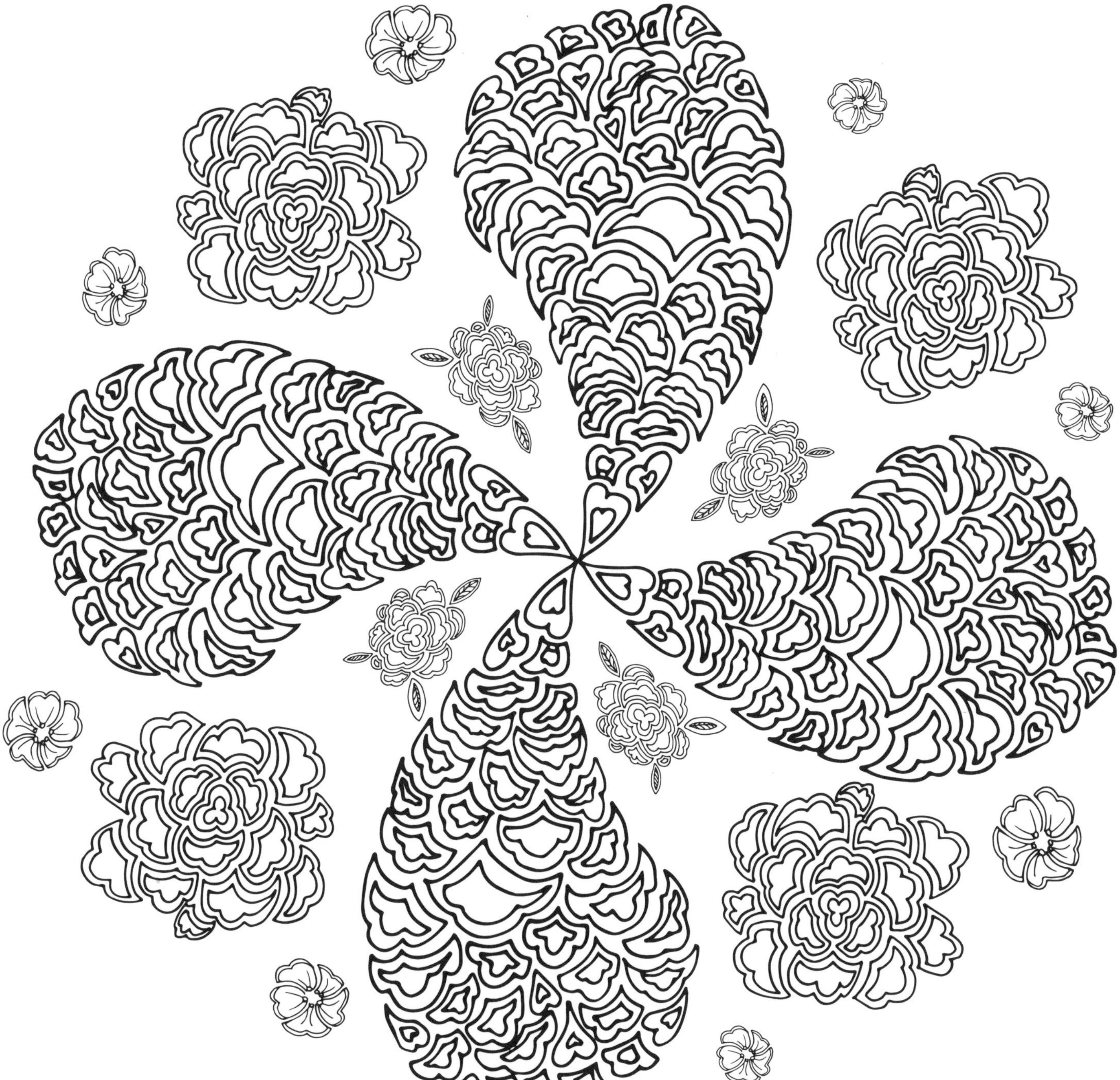

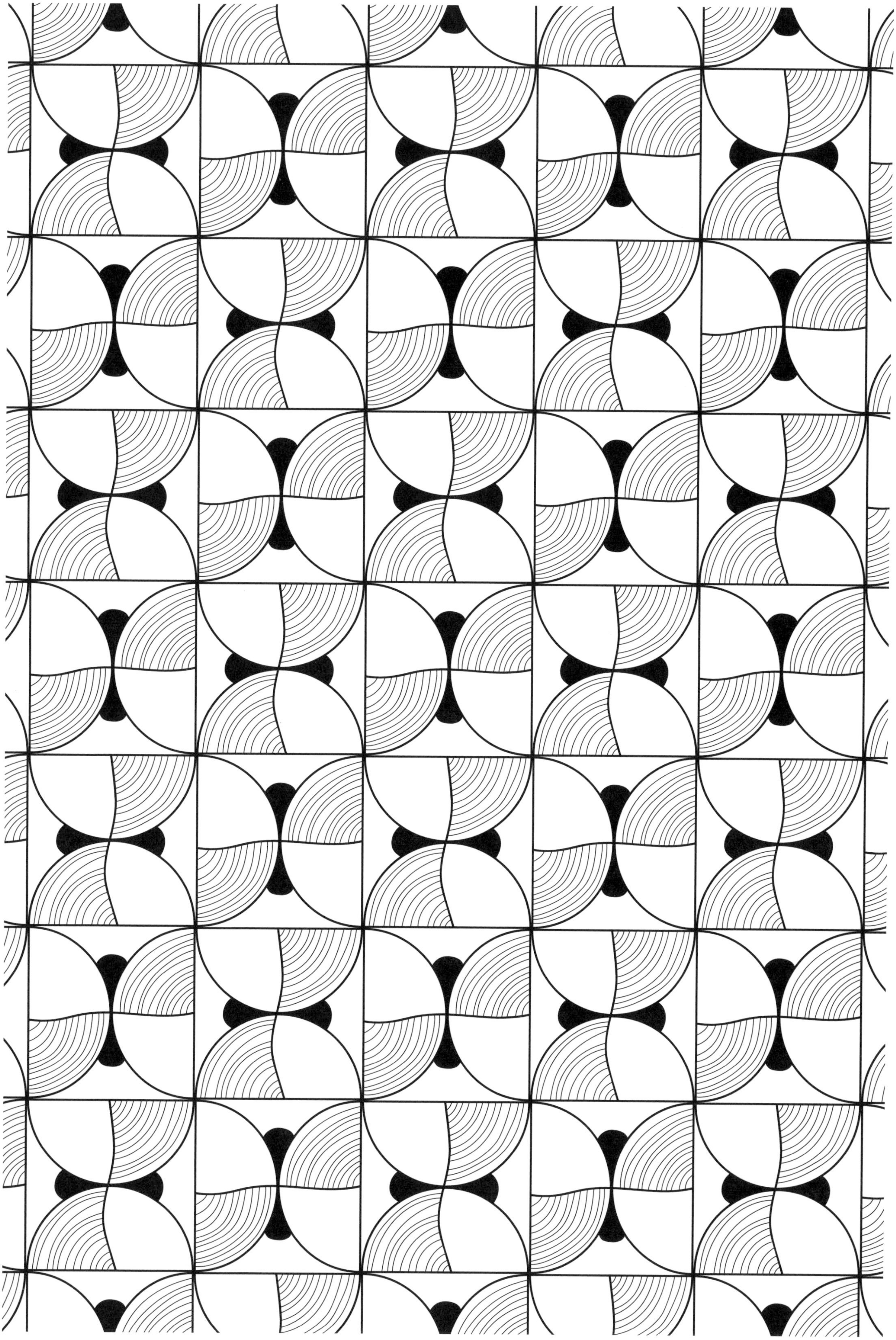

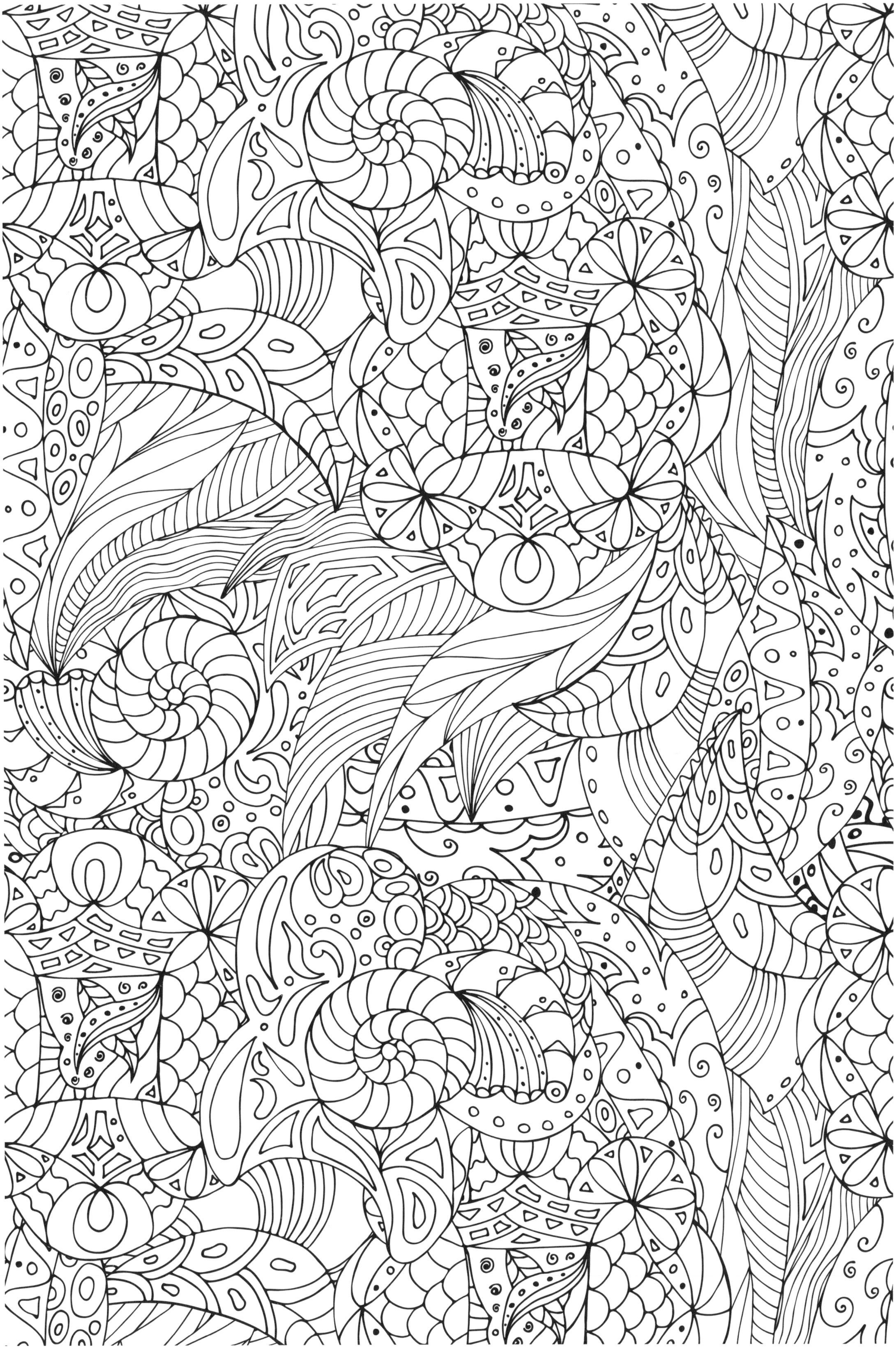

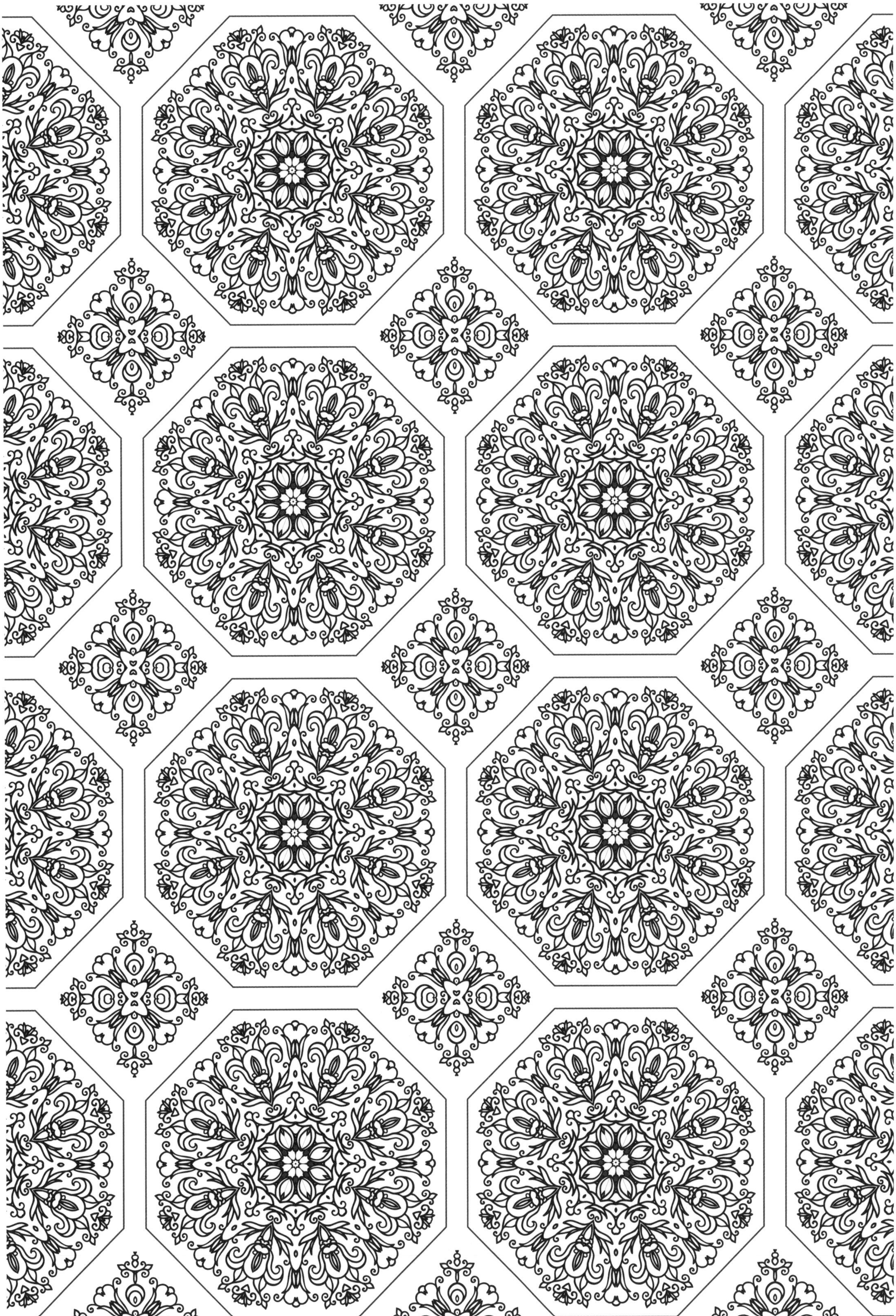

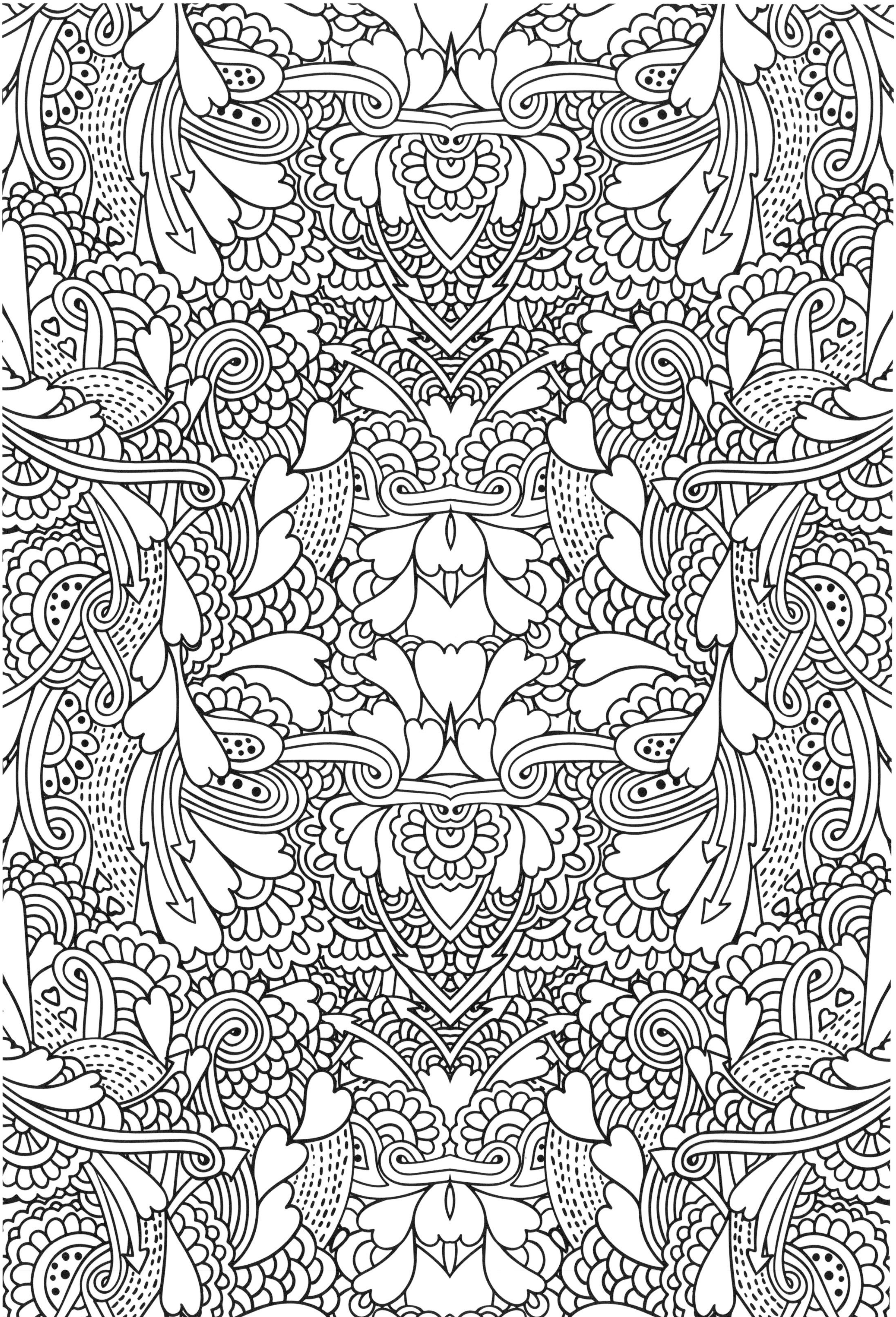

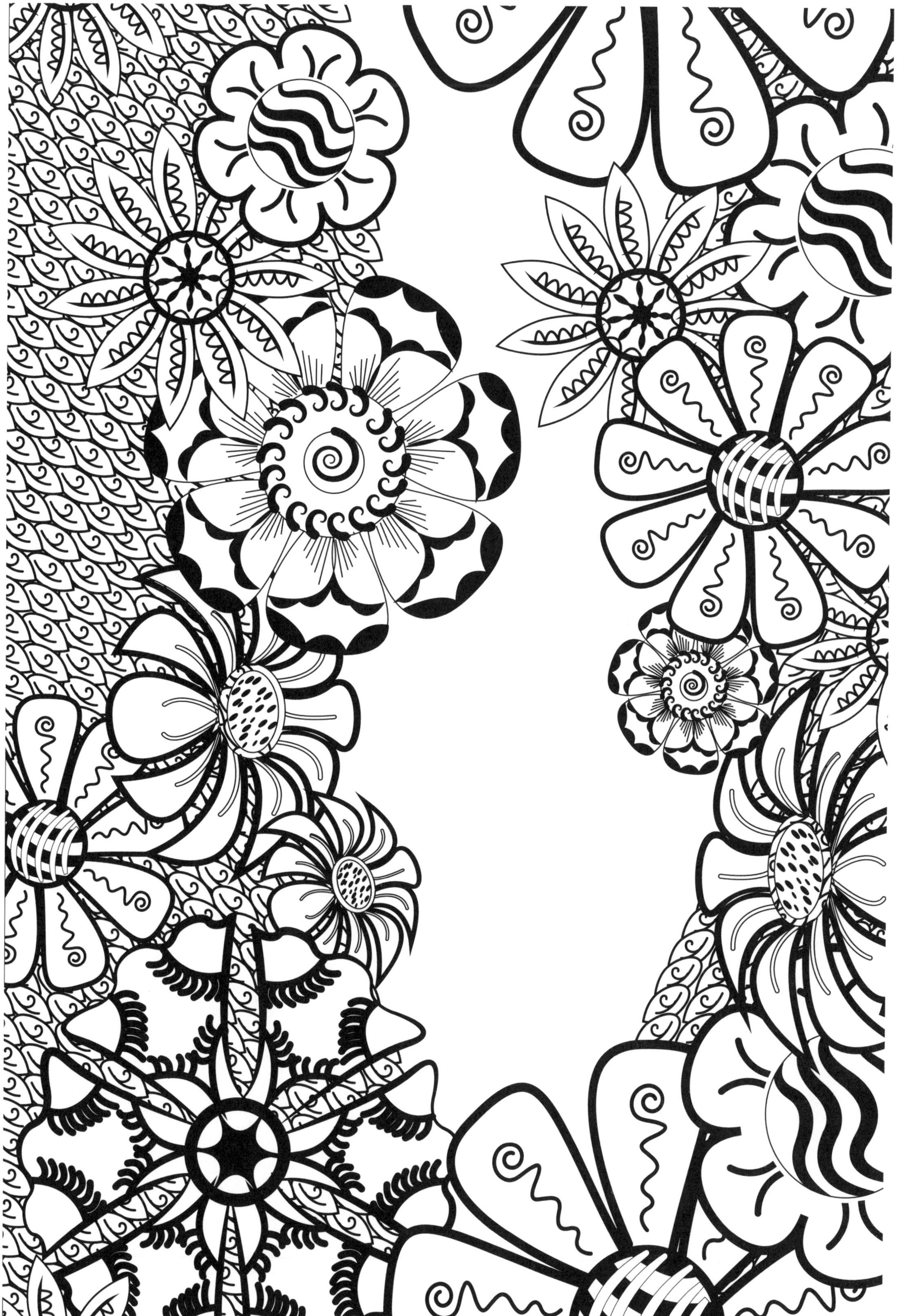

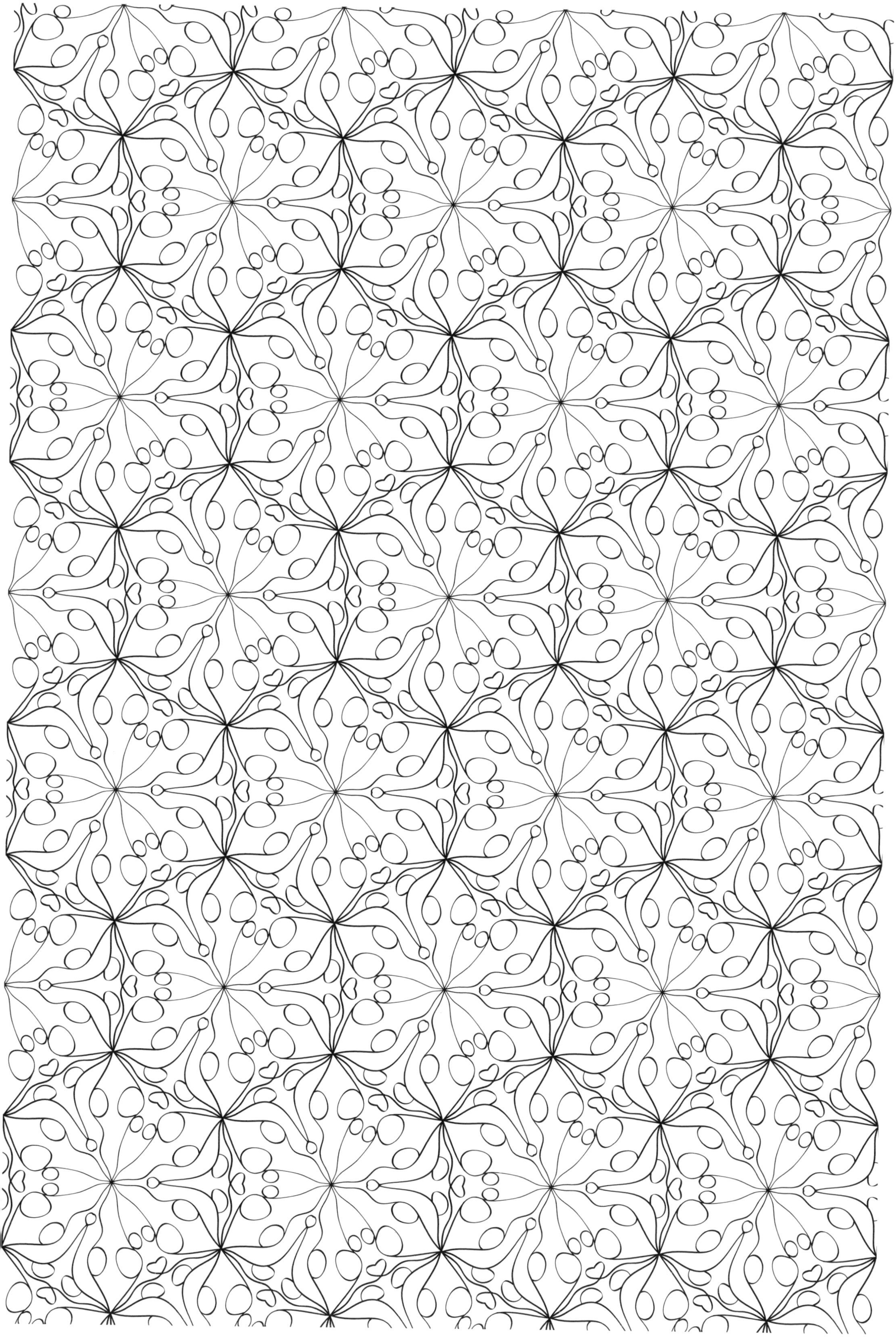

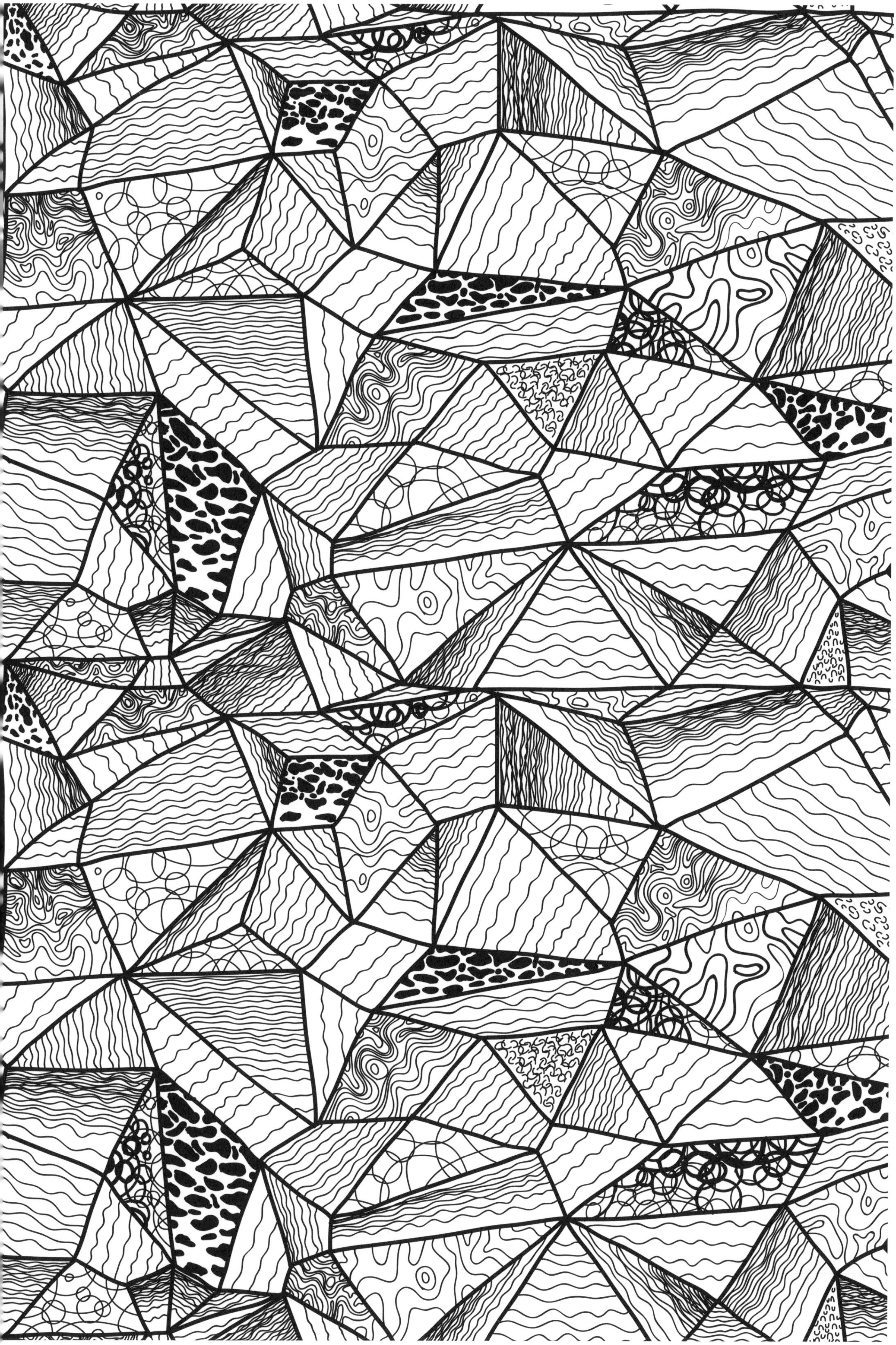

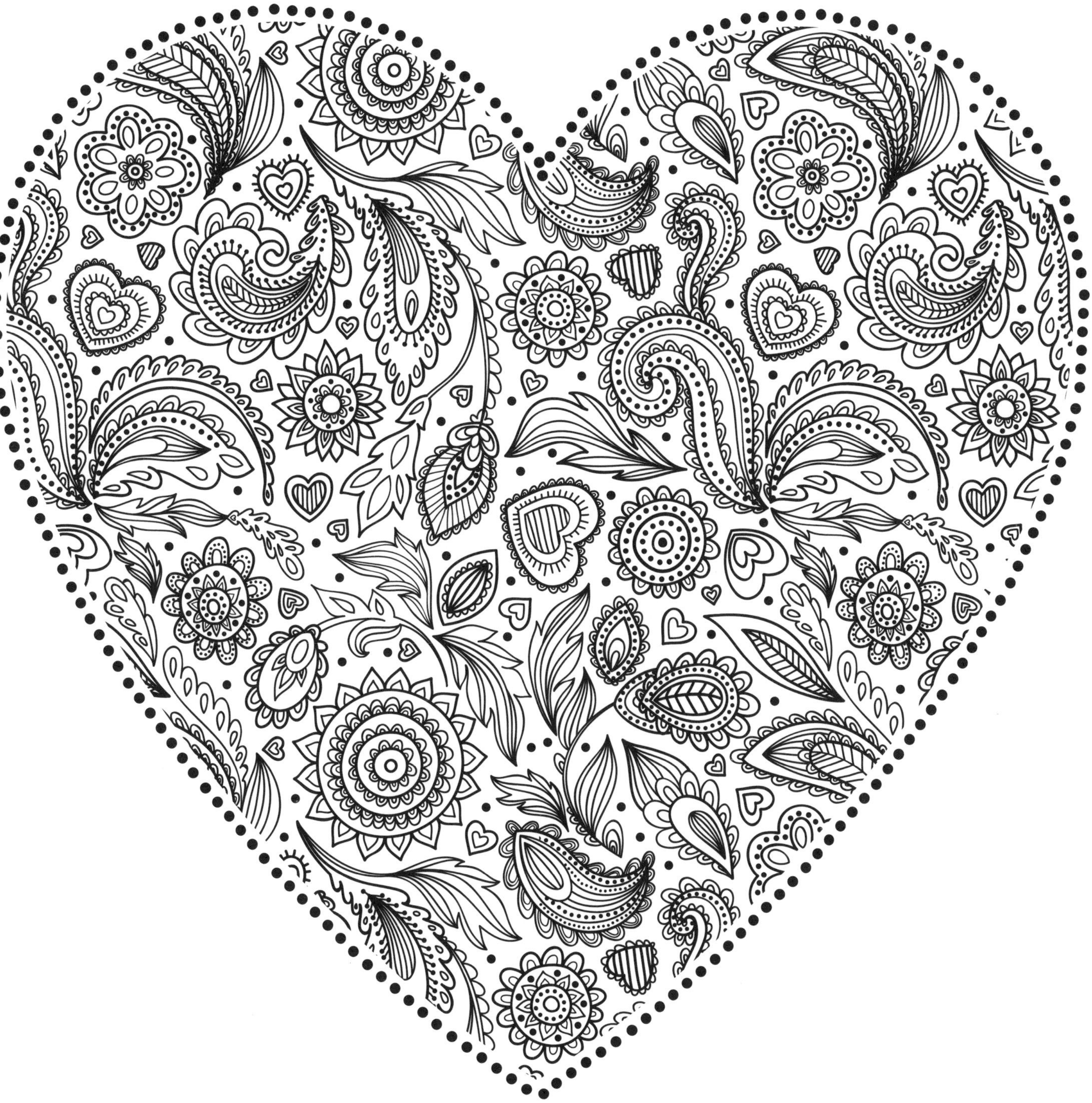

To place an order, or to request a catalog, contact:

GMC Publications Ltd,
Castle Place, 166 High Street,
Lewes, East Sussex, BN7 1XU,
United Kingdom

Tel: +44 (0)1273 488005

www.gmcbooks.com

All images provided by Shutterstock, Inc.